CURRICULUM LINKS

ages 5-7

Plants and animals

Suzanne Kirk

Credits

Author
Suzanne Kirk

Editor
Dulcie Booth

Assistant editor
Roanne Charles

Series designer
Lynne Joesbury

Designer
Catherine Mason

Illustrations
Terry Burton

Cover photograph
© The Garden Picture Library/Alamy

Photographic symbols
Art & design © Stockbyte. Science and citizenship © Ingram Publishing.

Published by Scholastic Ltd,
Villiers House,
Clarendon Avenue,
Leamington Spa,
Warwickshire
CV32 5PR
Printed by Bell & Bain Ltd, Glasgow
Text © Suzanne Kirk
© 2004 Scholastic Ltd
1 2 3 4 5 6 7 8 9 0   4 5 6 7 8 9 0 1 2 3

Visit our website at www.scholastic.co.uk

British Library Cataloguing-in-Publication Data
A catalogue record for this book is available from
the British Library.

ISBN 0-439-97120-9

Contents

Acknowledgements

Photographs
pages 5, 11, 15, 18, 24, 29, 32 and 53
© Photodisc, Inc.
pages 8, 17 and 41 © Ingram Publishing
pages 23, 51 and 57 © Nova Developments
page 31 © 2004/Steve Bloom Images/
alamy.com
page 36 © Stockbyte
page 47 © Eyewire
page 58 © Getty Images/Yuri Shibnev

Introduction

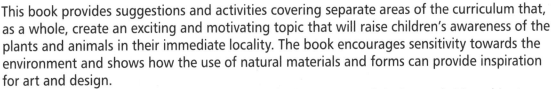

This book provides suggestions and activities covering separate areas of the curriculum that, as a whole, create an exciting and motivating topic that will raise children's awareness of the plants and animals in their immediate locality. The book encourages sensitivity towards the environment and shows how the use of natural materials and forms can provide inspiration for art and design.

Plants and animals brings together aspects of science, art and design and citizenship. It will help you to present an interesting and relevant topic at Key Stage 1 over a number of weeks, enabling the children to investigate and explore, to observe, to draw and to develop ideas for their own designs and create collaborative and individual works of art. There are opportunities for fieldwork, first-hand observation and science investigation.

Generally, the activities in each section of *Plants and animals* follow on progressively. In section 1, the activities develop through the experience of fieldwork. Section 2 culminates with the making of a class collage. After an introduction to seeds, the activities of section 3 follow the procedures for a scientific investigation. The activities of section 4 help children create an individual fabric collage, while section 5 provides a sequence of activities to develop aspects of citizenship, encouraging interest and participation in a school wildlife area. Section 6 focuses on the reproduction of familiar animals.

What subject areas are covered?

This book covers the QCA science unit 2B, 'Plants and animals in the local environment', art and design unit 2B 'Mother Nature, designer' and citizenship unit 3, 'Animals and us'. At this stage children's experience of the world around them is increasing rapidly. This topic aims to develop their natural curiosity through observation and personal experience of their immediate surroundings. They are encouraged to look closely, to discover and to learn to respect the plants and animals with which they share their environment. They will discover how plants and animals have always provided a multitude of inspirational ideas when designing and creating works of art. Developing a child's awareness and curiosity of plants and animals at this stage, can lead to a lifelong respect for, interest in and fascination with the natural world.

© Photodisc, Inc.

Teaching specific subject areas through a topic

While it is important to distinguish between the separate subject areas of science, art and design and citizenship, natural links can be difficult to ignore and in fact are extremely useful in relating one area of work to another. One subject focus can provide an opportunity to explore in more than one field.

A carefully planned topic can meld together prescribed areas of the curriculum to create interesting learning experiences appropriate to the needs of the class. Topic-based work presents a whole picture, motivates children and encourages their enthusiasm.

Getting started

Familiarise yourself with the area around the school and search out local sites for fieldwork opportunities. These could be within the school grounds or close by so that several excursions are possible. Ensure that the sites are safe, free from contamination and provide relevant opportunities for first-hand experience and investigation.

Check out any designated wildlife areas within the school grounds. Find out how they are managed, talk to the children and staff involved and be aware of the behaviour code to be followed by children visiting the sites. If there is nowhere set aside for wildlife, consider developing a special site with the help of children and parents. This could be a simple feeding station for birds, a beetle bank and log pile, a garden or area of shrubs, or a patch of ground that is not mown, allowing grass to grow tall and wildflowers to flourish.

Begin a collection of pictures, fabrics, furnishings and household items that show examples of design inspired by natural materials.

Involving parents

Involving parents and carers is a useful strategy in helping to motivate children during their topic work. Prepare a letter to parents and carers outlining the areas of work in which their children will be involved. Encourage them to listen to their children who will want to share their experiences as they become involved in outdoor discoveries, science investigation, developing a respect for their environment and designing and making activities.

Explain that excursions will take place, and request information on any problems this might raise with individual children, including potential allergies from plants or soil. Take this opportunity to ask for extra adult helpers if appropriate. Helpers might also be required for assisting with groups during art activities. Inform parents of plans for a wildlife area and encourage their help and suggestions.

Point out that children might like to continue working on their ideas at home. Their curiosity for wildlife when out and about should be encouraged, as should any interest in the immediate surroundings of their own garden or mini wildlife area. Children might want to practise newly learnt skills such as sewing, drawing and gluing, and produce further artwork.

Resources

Collect pictures and books on a range of local plants including trees, flowers, seedlings, moss, also garden flowers and vegetables; a range of animals found locally, including small mammals, farm animals, birds, minibeasts; familiar pets; designs based on naturals forms.

Build up collections of natural materials, particularly non-perishable items that can be collected in advance, such as dried leaves, cones, pebbles and stones, pieces of wood and bark; fresh products: fruits and flowers; seeds: acorns, conkers, ash and sycamore keys, honesty seed cases and sunflower heads, peas and beans, grass seed and grain, packets of seeds, poppy heads; fabric and household items showing designs inspired by natural forms.

Try to collect as many of the following as possible:

■ for fieldwork: clipboards, plastic bags, small trowels, magnifying aids
■ for scientific investigation: shallow containers or small transparent tubs, peat-free compost, cling film, absorbent material such as towelling or kitchen paper, plant pots
■ for artwork: thin card or thick drawing paper, different textures of plain and patterned paper, such as wallpaper samples, birthday cards, wrapping paper, packaging; a selection of fabrics, some for backgrounds, such as hessian or felt, others for collage work, including a range of plain ones, patterns, colours and textures
■ sewing threads, embellishments such as beads, buttons, ribbons, sequins and so on, scissors, large-eyed needles, pins
■ plastic folders and boxes for storage
■ pet accessories, such as feeding and drinking equipment, dog leads, food labels

■ plant material, which could include growing a tomato plant in a pot and sowing seeds of honesty, poppies and teasels in a patch of garden providing examples of seeds and demonstrating the life cycles of flowering plants year after year
■ still and video cameras
■ a wildlife area within the school grounds – consult your county's Wildlife Trust for information and advice.

Fieldwork opportunities

Fieldwork is an essential part of this topic if children are to appreciate the world around them and develop an awareness of the range of plants and animals that share their environment. Working out of doors encourages children to notice and observe, to ask questions, form opinions and make decisions. Through first-hand experience of the lives of plants and animals, children can be encouraged to develop a respect for the natural world. Fieldwork should be purposeful and enjoyable. Children are understandably excited about leaving the classroom but should appreciate that fieldwork is school work in a different environment, where they can explore, observe and discover things for themselves.

   Section 1 requires children to look for the different plants and animals living in the locality. They also need to collect natural materials as a stimulus for their artwork. In section 2 children examine different habitats to discover the types of plants and animals to be found there. There are opportunities to focus on conservation of local environments. Section 3 provides opportunities for children to look closely at flowering plants to discover the development of seeds. Section 5 involves children taking an active part in a school wildlife area, which could become a valuable resource. They can be encouraged to extend their interest to the plants and animals of their own gardens. In section 6 children are encouraged to observe the development of young animals. They can discover the eggs and caterpillars of moths and butterflies, recognise young farm animals and watch out for nesting birds. Sensitivity towards all animals is encouraged. Through fieldwork in all sections there are valuable opportunities to encourage respect for wildlife.

   The school grounds often provide valuable opportunities for fieldwork. Excursions beyond the school gates need to be very carefully organised:
■ Enlist extra help from other adults so that children can be cared for in small groups.
■ Plan the excursion in detail. Brief all helpers thoroughly. Make sure they are aware of the route to be taken and are clear about procedures for crossing roads.
■ Make sure the children are well informed about the purpose of the fieldwork, what they are expected to look out for, any recording they will need to do and the behaviour expected of them. Remind them about safety issues, particularly involving traffic. Insist they stay close to the adult leader of their group. Emphasise the need for respect of the environment at all times.
■ Carry with you a basic first aid kit, extra pencils and paper and a mobile phone.
■ Suggest suitable clothing, ensuring the children have hats and gloves when it is cold or sunhats and rainwear as appropriate. Encourage suitable footwear for brisk walking.
■ Check school and LEA guidelines for off-site visits.

Introducing the topic to children

Present this topic as an exciting area of work for both the children and yourself, with lots of things to look forward to. Explain that the topic involves finding out lots of information about their local environment, especially the plants and animals that are all around them. There will be opportunities to work out of doors, to investigate and make discoveries, to build up collections, to draw, create designs and produce works of art as a class and individually.

Starting points

Elicit the children's initial responses on plants and animals before starting the topic. Ask what plants they have growing in their gardens. Do they think there are many different animals living in their neighbourhood? Do they know of any wild places nearby where plants and animals might be living? Where is their favourite outdoor place to go?

Section 1

Plants and animals in the local environment

FOCUS

SCIENCE

SCIENCE
- exploring, observing and drawing natural materials
- plants and animals of the local environment
- fieldwork opportunities and first-hand observations
- recording and communicating information discovered

CITIZENSHIP
- care and respect for animals, including minibeasts
- developing ground rules for wildlife areas

CITIZENSHIP

ART AND DESIGN
- materials and designs in nature

ART & DESIGN

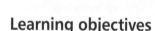

SCIENCE   CITIZENSHIP

ACTIVITY 1

PLANTS AROUND US

Learning objectives
To be aware of different types of plants in the locality through fieldwork; to encourage sensitivity towards local environments.

Resources
For fieldwork – photocopiable page 19; clipboards and pencils; magnifying aids; camera. For classroom work – books about common plants; pencils and crayons; photocopiable page 19.

Preparation
Locate an area where the children can safely look for plants in their immediate environment. This could be within the school grounds, otherwise an excursion to a nearby park or wild area might need to be arranged. Plan a route along which children can see a variety of plants including trees, grass, weeds and perhaps garden flowers and vegetable plants. Find a suitable stopping place where closer examination of plants can take place. Although many plants can be poisonous or irritants, be aware of any especially harmful species to be encountered locally. Avoid areas contaminated by dog faeces, litter and other dangerous rubbish. If leaving the school premises, refer to the school policy and LEA guidelines for off-site visits. Inform parents of any planned excursion and ensure the children have suitable footwear and clothing. (See Fieldwork opportunities, page 7). Enlist extra adults so that the children can work in small groups during the activity.

© Ingram Publishing

Activity

Tell the children that they will be taking part in an outdoor lesson during which they will need to make very careful observations of the plants which are growing in the neighbourhood. Point out that they will not be picking any of the plants but will be using their sense of sight to discover what kinds of plants there are and where they like to grow. Warn against any poisonous or irritant plants likely to be encountered. Make sure the children know when the activity will take place, what they will need, who will be looking after them and how they are expected to behave as well as the objective of the fieldwork.

Put the children into small groups. Provide the leaders of the groups with photocopiable page 19. Explain that during the outdoor lesson, each group will search for examples to include on the sheet.

Take the children along to the fieldwork area. Start by asking them to look around and tell you what plants they recognise. Advise them to move around in a sensitive manner so as to make as little impact on the area as possible. The children will probably point out grass, flowers and weeds, bushes and trees. Give clues as necessary to help them cover the range of plants. Choose some common species to identify such as holly, horsechestnut or sycamore, dandelion, daisy or thistle, a patch of moss. Look for areas of short and longer grass. Provide magnifying aids for looking at the details of plants. Point out that there are many plants which they (and you) probably do not know the names of. Explain that there must be hundreds of different plants growing round about and it is not possible to know the names of all of them. However, they are all important – many of them providing food for animals.

In their groups, ask the children to provide suggestions for the leader to record on the photocopiable sheet. The largest plants to be seen will probably be trees, some of which it might be possible to name, the smallest an unidentifiable seedling or strand of moss. They can provide several ideas for the most interesting plant and try to find a plant which is growing in an unusual place; perhaps in a crack in a wall or pushing its way through a path. Encourage several examples to be recorded where appropriate. Take photographs of the area generally and to record the discoveries the children make, for example children standing next to a tall tree or other large plant; a child holding a coin or ruler next to a very small specimen; a plant growing on a log or stone; a plant with colourful flowers or unusual leaves. Before leaving the area, check with the children that no litter has been left and praise them for making very little impression on their surroundings while they worked.

Draw the children's attention to cultivated plants in gardens along the route or in the school grounds if these types of plants were absent from the area where the main part of the activity took place.

Recording

Back in the classroom, provide the children with their own copies of photocopiable page 19. They can use the fieldwork notes to help with remembering when making their own recording. If necessary, read the headings and discuss how the observations and discoveries can be presented. Encourage the children to make drawings and write relevant words or phrases. Where a plant has not been identified, a simple description can be included – *a plant taller than me with a thick stem and white flowers*. Point out that it is important to include the date so that they will know when the observations took place.

Differentiation

Children:
■ recognise a range of plants, recording examples as drawings; developing sensitivity towards the environment
■ recognise and identify different plants, recording specific examples by drawing and labels; show sensitivity towards the environment
■ are aware of the different plants in the locality, recording a range of examples as drawings and notes; begin to understand the importance of sensitive behaviour in the environment.

Plants and animals in the local environment

Plenary

In pairs, ask the children to name or describe ten plants between them that they remember from this activity, using their fingers to help them. Then begin a class list to which children can add other plants they see around them. Did they think they would find so many? Emphasise the range of sizes from the tallest tree to the smallest grass seedling. Suggest the children use books to find out more about the plants they have seen around their neighbourhood. Talk about how important it is to avoid damaging plants in parks and wild areas.

Display

Arrange books and pictures of common plants together with any labelled photographs taken during the fieldwork. Dig up a dandelion plant and display it in a jar of water so the children can see the root as well as the leaves and flower.

SCIENCE

CITIZENSHIP

ACTIVITY 2

ANIMALS AROUND US

Learning objectives

To observe the range of animals in the immediate environment; to recognise hazards when working with soil; to encourage sensitivity towards minibeasts.

Resources

For fieldwork: magnifying aids, small trowel, camera, clipboards, paper and pencils; photocopiable page 20; pencils and crayons for classroom recording; pictures of minibeasts the children are likely to see including earthworm, spider, insects and so on.

Preparation

Find locations in the school grounds where the children will be able to observe animals for themselves. Perhaps create a trail so that the children observe at predetermined spots. For example, choose a spot from where children can observe a wide area and see the most noticeable animals such as cats, dogs, birds and humans, also perhaps butterflies and bees. Look for an area with clues that show small creatures such as insects live there but are perhaps hidden, such as nibbled leaves and gnawed stones from cherry trees. Find a wall or corner of a building where there are spiders and other small animals living in cracks and holes.

Several days before the activity, arrange some pieces of stone or wood in an undisturbed but easily accessible place and check before you take the children out that there are creatures to be discovered there. These might include woodlice, beetles and slugs.

Decide upon an area of suitable soil, perhaps a garden border where it is possible to dig to investigate animals in the soil. Make sure the area is free from any contamination such as dog and cat faeces or glass.

Activity

Take the children outside the building and ask them to look out for any animals they might see. They might expect to see a cat or dog, or perhaps farm animals if the location is suitable. Begin a list of the animals the children identify and take photographs, if possible. Then remind the children that all creatures are animals and encourage them to spot birds perching and flying. Remind them that humans too are animals. Move on to ask the children where they think there might be very small animals close by. Help the children to notice clues so that they begin to realise there are minibeasts hiding away in different habitats all around them.

For example, look for nibbled leaves of plants which indicate that animals are living close by.
If there is a suitable wall, help the children to spot the animals living there, such as spiders, beetles and perhaps woodlice. Encourage them to use magnifying aids, if appropriate, and point out that the animals should not be disturbed. Next, show the children the pieces of stone/wood you placed earlier and lift these carefully to reveal the small animals living there. Insist that the stones are replaced so that the animals can continue living relatively undisturbed. Then, using a small trowel, dig an area of soft soil to reveal any creatures living there, including earthworms. While observing the smaller creatures, remind the children that these animals share the environment with larger animals such as themselves and all of them should be allowed the opportunity to continue living undisturbed as much as possible. Do not encourage the children to touch and disturb the animals at this stage and demonstrate careful handling if you need to give the children a closer look at any of the creatures such as the earthworm.

Point out that after working out of doors hands must be washed on returning to the building. Explain that there are germs also living in the soil that can cause illness if they get inside our bodies. Talk about not licking dirty fingers and the importance of always washing hands before eating.

Recording
Back in the classroom, show the children photocopiable page 20 and ask them to draw the animals that were seen. Point out where they should include any of the animals seen above the ground and where those that hide away can be shown. Write the names of the animals that were observed on a board or flip chart or photocopy the list for pairs of children to share. They can then label the observed animals they have drawn. Remind the children to include the date to show when the animals were seen.

Differentiation
Children:
■ recognise different animals in the immediate environment; begin to show sensitivity towards small creatures; are aware of health hazards when working out of doors
■ recognise and identify a range of animals in the immediate environment; show sensitivity towards small creatures; understand health hazards when working out of doors
■ are aware that there is a wide range of animals in the immediate environment; begin to understand the need for sensitivity towards small creatures and the hazards to health when working out of doors.

Plenary
Talk about the range of animals observed. Describe one of the animals and ask the children if they can identify it, for example *We found this animal living under a stone. It has many legs.* Encourage the children to describe animals for the rest of the class to name. Ask the children to remind each other why it is important to avoid disturbing small animals, as well as the need to wash hands after fieldwork.

Display
Arrange pictures and photographs of any animals observed, perhaps grouping them into 'large' and 'small' or 'above ground' and 'below ground'. If space allows, create a frieze with children's drawings and appropriate labels, which demonstrates animals living above and below ground.

© Photodisc, Inc.

SCIENCE

ACTIVITY 3

PRESENTING RESULTS IN A CHART

Plants and animals in the local environment

Learning objective
To record observed plants and animals in a chart.

Resources
Board or flip chart; thin card; paper; pencils.

Presenting results in a chart	
plants	where we found them

animals	where we found them

Preparation
The children will need to have observed the plants and animals of the surrounding area as in the previous two activities so the information they have collected can be collated as a chart/table. Prepare the framework of the intended chart on the board (see left) and on recording sheet for the children. Make cards on which the locations are written, such as *under a stone, among leaves, in the hedgerow, along the road*. Reserve some blank cards for the children's suggestions.

Activity
Talk to the children about the plants and animals they have observed during the fieldwork of the previous two activities. Remind them of the range of plants and animals they discovered. Did the children think they would find so many different types of these living things? Point out that other people might be interested to know what can be found in this particular neighbourhood and it would be useful to find a way of presenting the information so that others could see what has been observed. Talk to the children about ways of recording information. Explain that a chart, which might also be called a table, is a useful means of presenting information that can be seen at a glance. Refer to any charts the children are already familiar with so they can begin to understand how such information can be displayed.

Show the children the framework of the chart you have prepared for the information about plants. Tell them that this can be used to record the names of the plants and where they were found. Point out the two columns, explaining that the boxes in the smaller one are for the names of the plants that were observed. Ask the children to provide the names of some of the plants they can remember, and write these in the chart. Then, taking each plant in turn, ask where it was found. For example, a daisy might have been found on the school field, and a horse chestnut tree in the park. Write in the children's suggestions or attach the prepared cards to the appropriate box.

Similarly, build up a chart to include some of the animals observed. Consider the children's suggestions and decide which is the best description of where they were seen.

Recording
Provide the children with their own copies of the framework for the chart that you prepared earlier. Explain where they should fill in the names of any plants they observed and point

out the boxes in which to write where they saw them. Refer to the examples written on the cards which they can use to help with ideas and spelling. Indicate the section of the table for recording the animals and where they were observed. Some children might like to produce a comprehensive record on a chart they have made themselves, to include all the plants and animals they have observed.

Differentiation
Children:
■ recognise a chart and are aware of its purpose; complete a chart using simple phrases
■ begin to understand the purpose of a chart; complete a chart using information they have collected
■ understand the purpose of a chart; can devise and complete a chart to communicate information collected.

Plenary
Ask some questions which require the children to use the information collected on a chart: *Where was a thistle found? Which animals were observed on the school field?* If appropriate, suggest the children take home a copy of the chart framework and record the plants and animals they observe in their own garden.

Display
Make a large chart framework into which children can write examples of their observations using coloured pens and including any new sightings.

ACTIVITY 4

WHERE PLANTS AND ANIMALS ARE FOUND

SCIENCE

Learning objective
To use experience gained from fieldwork to identify plants and animals and where they are found.

Resources
Photocopiable page 21; pencils.

Preparation
The children will need to have observed the plants and animals living in their local environment.

Activity
Tell the children you have a riddle for them to solve. Explain that a riddle is a kind of puzzle that provides clues that can be used to help work out the answer. Ask the children to listen carefully and think about all the clues, but not to share their ideas until everyone has had time to think.

Present the class with a riddle that describes one of the animals they have observed in the locality, pausing between each statement to allow time for thinking. This could be: *I am very small. I have eight legs. I can dangle from a thread of silk. What am I and where can you find me?* The children should easily guess that the creature is a spider. Encourage them to remember the places where they found spiders when they were making their own observations. Move on to a riddle that describes a familiar plant, such as a tree the children know well: *I am taller than a house. I am also very old. I do not move about.* Provide an extra clue relating to a specific tree that the children have observed. Then ask, *What am I and where can you find me?*

Provide further riddles for the children to solve or ask them to think of their own.

Recording

Show the children photocopiable page 21 on which there are riddles to solve. If appropriate, read them through and work on a couple of examples. Remind the children what they are trying to find out and where to write their answers. On the reverse of the page children can write riddles they have devised themselves.

Differentiation

Children:
■ identify some familiar plants and animals from clues
■ identify and record a range of familiar plants and animals from clues; with help devise riddles of their own
■ identify and record a wide range of plants and animals from clues, devising accurate examples of their own.

Plenary

Encourage some children to read out their own riddles for the rest of the class to solve. Perhaps some children have described the same plant or animal with different clues. Point out that some plants or animals might be found in more than one place. For example, a robin can be seen perching in a tree or pecking food from the ground. Talk about how a collection of clues can lead you to the right answer.

Display

Compile a book of riddles that the children can read and solve.

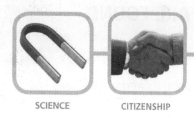

SCIENCE   CITIZENSHIP

ACTIVITY 5

SENSITIVITY TOWARDS PLANTS AND ANIMALS

Learning objective

To understand that humans have a responsibility to all plants and animals, especially those sharing our immediate environment.

Resources

Prepared sheets divided into three or five boxes for the children's recording.

Preparation

The children will need to have observed the plants and animals of their locality as in the previous activities.

Activity

Remind the children about their search for animals that live round about. Point out that these creatures share the environment with human animals, including themselves. They need somewhere to live; they need to be able to find a food supply. Briefly distinguish between those animals such as pets which are cared for by humans (did the children observe any cats and dogs?) and the majority which need to be left alone so they can live an undisturbed life.

Talk about how important it was to take care when looking for minibeasts (see activity 2, page 10). Ask the children to remind each other what steps were taken to ensure small animals were not injured or disturbed unnecessarily while the class was engaged in fieldwork, how the stones were lifted and replaced carefully to avoid harming any creatures living there. Ask if any of the children can think why it is not a good idea to leave the animals exposed for too long. Perhaps they will suggest the animals prefer to hide away, do not like bright sunlight, prefer to live in dark, shady places.

Move on to ways in which animals can be helped and encouraged to live in our environment. Have the children any ideas? Perhaps at home they put out food for birds or have plants in their garden which attract bees and butterflies. Make a link between the plants observed growing in the environment and the animals that rely on them for food and shelter. Talk about litter and the ill effects it can have on wildlife. Encourage the children to develop positive attitudes towards all living things. Explain why it is important to look after trees and other plants rather than wilfully damaging them and to avoid disturbing or harming wild animals. Explain what it means to have a responsibility towards other living creatures and how we all should respect the plants and animals that share the environment with us.

© Photodisc, Inc.

Recording

Suggest the children devise an individual code for themselves, perhaps with three or five points to show their responsibility towards animals and plants. Points could include such statements as: *I will put out food for the birds in winter; I will take care not to tread on spiders; I will ask my family to help me put some plants in the garden for birds and small animals.*

Show the children the layout of the sheet where they can write and illustrate three to five ideas for a personal code.

Differentiation

Children:
■ begin to develop a respect for the plants and animals of the local environment; record a code using drawings
■ show respect for plants and animals of the local environment; record this using drawings and simple sentences
■ begin to understand the importance of sensitivity towards plants and animals of the local environment; record this using drawings, relevant headings and sentences.

Plenary

Ask some of the children to read out their code statements. Comment on really good ideas. Remind the children that plants and animals are an important part of their environment and that, as humans, we can do many things to help other living things survive.

Display

Write or print out a selection of the code statements covering as many relevant aspects as possible. Display these prominently.

ART & DESIGN

CITIZENSHIP

ACTIVITY 6

COLLECTING NATURAL MATERIALS

Learning objectives
To explore natural materials from the local environment; to develop respect for the local environment

Resources
Hand lenses; camera; plastic bags; a suitable area where children can look for dead natural materials; pieces of card or paper on which to arrange the collections.

Preparation
Locate a suitable place where the children can safely collect dead and decaying natural materials. This could be a nearby park or garden, along a country footpath, or a small copse. Children living near the sea will be able to include materials from the seashore. Ensure the area is free from contamination by litter, animal faeces or other dangerous materials. Inform parents by letter of the day of the visit and the type of clothing and footwear the children will need. Organise extra adult helpers so that the children can work together in small groups. Check school and LEA health and safety guidelines.

Activity
Beforehand, talk to the children about the purpose of their outing – that they will be searching for materials to help them with an art and design activity. Explain that the items they are looking for must be natural materials, such as parts of plants. The plant material must be dead; pieces of bark and twigs, fallen leaves and seed pods can be collected. Point out that it is not a good idea to take living parts of plants in the wild as the plant can be damaged. Pebbles and small pieces of stone can also be collected as these are natural materials from the earth. Avoid animal remains except for shells and feathers. Suggest the children are selective as they search, considering the interest of each piece they collect, asking themselves why they like it rather than just collecting in quantity.

Provide the children with a plastic bag each and take them to the chosen area. Start them off by choosing something and describing its qualities, for example *I like this cone which I found under this tree. It is spiky and if you look closely you can see seeds inside. This leaf skeleton is very delicate. The veins make interesting patterns.*

Allow the children time to browse and make their selections. Talk about the range of things they are able to find. Emphasise the tactile qualities of some of the finds, for example *Sam has found a very smooth pebble.*

Back at school, point out the importance of hand washing after searching through leaf litter and so on. Then talk to the children about examining their collections and

arranging them on a piece of card. Perhaps demonstrate this with your own collection: *I think I will put this piece of twig next to these leaves which I have arranged in an overlapping pattern. I will try this pebble towards the edge of the design.* Allow time for the children to make their individual arrangements. Give advice where appropriate, but always encourage the children's own ideas. Take photographs of each design if possible and, if space allows, position them so they can be viewed if only for a short time.

Differentiation
Children:
■ collect and arrange natural materials
■ collect natural materials selectively and make an individual arrangement
■ choose natural materials selectively and arrange them to produce an imaginative design.

Recording
If appropriate, children can photograph their own arrangement and write an appropriate heading.

Plenary
Remind the children of the range of material they were able to collect. Talk about the arrangements. Point out those that are particularly successful, perhaps where similar items have been grouped together or the space has been used sensibly. However point out that there is no wrong way of arranging things, that each arrangement is special to the person who worked on it. Encourage the children to express their opinions of each other's efforts sensitively.

Display
Display the arrangements for a short time, then use any photographs to demonstrate the children's efforts. Continue this activity by having a collection of suitable materials of which pairs of children make a new arrangement each day: *Today's design is by Sean and Alice.*

ACTIVITY 7

LOOKING CLOSELY

ART & DESIGN

Learning objective
To record natural materials from first-hand experience.

Resources
The children's collections of natural materials from the previous activity or a new collection which might include seed pods and flower heads from a garden, and unusual fruits and vegetables from a greengrocer's shop; magnifying aids; drawing paper, pencils, coloured pencils or pastels.

Preparation
Have available the materials from the children's collections from the previous activity.

Activity
Tell the children you would like them to look very closely at the items in their collection, (or the new collection that you have

provided) and to choose two of these things to draw. Suggest they spend a short time examining the items and then thinking carefully about the angle and position that they would like to draw. Provide magnifying aids and encourage the children to look for an interesting view or position before they begin to draw. Give help where appropriate, perhaps suggesting a line that can be used as a starting point or a pattern which can be followed. Discourage the children from wanting to erase large parts of a drawing, instead suggest a new drawing is made alongside the first attempt. Point out that every sketch they make is acceptable and that artists often make several drawings before they have one they are really satisfied with. Artists and designers also look back at their first attempts to see how their ideas have changed, so these should not be destroyed.

Depending on the material available and the interest of the individual, children can then make a drawing of the same item at a different angle, perhaps from above or by moving the item into a different position. Suggest some drawings are left as pencil sketches, especially ones with careful detail, while others can be softly coloured with pencil crayons or pastels.

Recording
Suggest the children make labels to accompany their observational drawings. These could be simple headings or explanatory sentences: *An interesting stone I found under a tree in the park.*

Differentiation
Children:
■ observe and make simple drawings of some chosen natural materials
■ choose from their collection of natural materials items to observe and draw
■ choose selectively from a collection of natural materials and make careful observational drawings.

Plenary
Select some of the drawings to talk about. Pick out an example where a child has made several drawings of the same item. Point out how interesting it is to see more than one attempt and that each time a drawing is made it will be different in some way. Identify care and detail as well as simple sketches. Explain that everyone has a different way of drawing, which is their own individual style.

Display
Emphasise the importance of the children's drawings by using special mounting and displaying them prominently. Use headings to communicate the importance of the individual designs.

© Photodisc, Inc.

SCIENCE   CITIZENSHIP

Photocopiable

Plants around us

What did you find?   Date: _____

> the largest

> the smallest

> the most colourful

> growing in unusual places

> the most interesting

Photocopiable

SCIENCE   CITIZENSHIP

Animals around us

Date: _____

animals living above the ground

animals living below the ground

SCHOLASTIC

Finding plants and animals

- My body is long and thin.
- I do not have legs
- I wriggle along when I move.

What am I?

_____

Where can you find me?

_____

- My leaves are like a lion's teeth.
- I have bright yellow flowers.
- Then I send seeds floating through the air.

What am I?

_____

Where can you find me?

_____

- I am usually grey or brownish.
- I hide away in the dark.
- I have seven pairs of legs.

What am I?

_____

Where can you find me?

_____

- Dark feathers cover my body.
- I fly and perch on trees and rooftops.
- My beak is golden.

What am I?

_____

Where can you find me?

_____

ST. MARY'S UNIVERSITY COLLEGE
A COLLEGE OF THE QUEEN'S UNIVERSITY OF BELFAST ■ SCHOLASTIC

Section 2

Our environment

FOCUS

SCIENCE
- identifying and comparing local habitats
- making and checking predictions
- sensitivity towards plants and animals in the local environment

SCIENCE

ART AND DESIGN
- observational drawings
- using natural materials to explore design ideas

ART & DESIGN

ACTIVITY 1

DIFFERENT HABITATS

SCIENCE

Learning objective
To be aware of different habitats within the local environment.

Resources
Paper, pencils and crayons.

Preparation
Familiarise yourself with the habitats around the school and if necessary those in the immediate neighbourhood with which the children are likely to be familiar. Make a list to refer to. Collect pictures of habitats, such as woodland, a hedgerow, pond and so on for display.

Activity
Remind the children of their observations of plants and animals during the fieldwork activities of section 1. Talk about plants and animals choosing to live in different places. For example, a bird would not be found under a stone and an earthworm would not choose to perch on a house roof. Explain that often plants and animals need very special places in which to survive. Although plants such as the dandelion seem to like to grow anywhere, a water lily, for example, will only grow in a pond or other watery place. Caterpillars need to live on plants while woodlice need to be in dark places.

Explain that a special area where a number of different plants and animals are able to live is called a habitat. Encourage the children to think of habitats around the school and together make a class list. Habitats could include a hedgerow, a garden area, the playing field, a pond, a patch of bare soil, the area around a tree, an old wall. If possible, include areas very close to the school which could be easily visited or with which the children are familiar, such as an open space, municipal garden, woodland, seashore, stream, and so on.

Move on to considering which of these habitats might provide homes for the greatest number of plants and animals. Perhaps encourage the children to think back to their fieldwork activities in section 1. Use different coloured pens to identify habitats where the children think they would find a large number of different plants and animals and those where they think there will be few living things trying to live and grow. Give clues if necessary: *There are lots of places to hide in the hedgerow/shrubbery, so as well as birds there might be lots of small animals living there. Because everyone plays on the grass, not many animals will be able to live there and other plants cannot survive. The river has so much rubbish in it that there will be very few animals living there.*

Recording
Ask the children to consider where they would expect to find the most and the fewest plants and animals and then list their top three habitats and the bottom three habitats.

Differentiation
Children:
■ are aware that there are different habitats and that they provide homes for plants and animals
■ recognise a range of local habitats and know that some provide homes for more plants and animals than others
■ identify a range of local habitats and begin to understand why some attract more species of plants and animals than others.

© Nova Developments

Plenary
Talk about the children's lists. Is there a habitat everyone agrees is a really good place for plants and animals to live? Similarly, do they generally agree on the habitat least likely to attract wildlife?

Display
Arrange pictures of common habitats with headings. Create a poster to show the habitats with a wide range of plants and animals and those with fewer species.

ACTIVITY 2

PLANTS AND ANIMALS IN DIFFERENT HABITATS

SCIENCE

Learning objective
To make predictions about the animals and plants found in different local habitats.

Resources
Photographs of plants and animals to be found living in local habitats; board or flip chart; paper; pencils.

Preparation
Choose two different habitats that are easily accessible and can be visited by the children in the following activity when they can check their predictions. One habitat should support a considerable population of plants and animals, such as a hedgerow or log pile and the second an area of bare ground beneath a tree or a section of a playing area where few species live. Make a note of the plants and animals in each habitat.

2

Our environment

Activity

Remind the children of the discussion about habitats in the previous activity. Make sure they understand that there are many different habitats and they are areas where plants can live and which also provide homes for several different types of animals. Talk about the nearby habitat you have chosen which supports a number of different plants and animals. Ask the children to think about what they will find living there and make a list of their ideas. Tell them that there will be an opportunity to check their predictions later. Offer clues and suggestions, referring to previous experience and fieldwork. *Do you think there might be very tiny plants living on the logs? What could they be?* This should prompt the children to remember the moss they have seen during observational fieldwork. Try to include a range of plants and animals, but it would be useful to leave some unmentioned for the children to discover when they check their predictions. Tick each species with a coloured pen or chalk to indicate that you expect to find these in the habitat.

Next, refer the children to the poorer habitat. Go through the list of plants and animals and decide whether each one would find a home in this second area. Use a different colour to highlight those the children predict they will find living there. Ask the children if they think there will be a plant or animal in this habitat that they are not likely to find in the first one. Add this to the list and colour-code it. Perhaps count the number of species in the original list and compare this number with the count for the second habitat.

Consider briefly why one habitat supports more life than another. Perhaps one provides more shelter and food than another; another is disturbed too much for many living things to survive there for long.

Recording

Suggest the children write relevant statements to declare their predictions for each habitat. For example, *Hedgerow – we think that there are many different plants and animals living in this habitat, such as…*

Differentiation

Children:
- are aware of differences in two local habitats and with help indicate on a chart which plants and animals might be found living there
- compare two different habitats; make and record predictions as to the plants and animals which might be found living there
- understand that there is a range of local habitats; predict and record the plants and animals which might be found in two different habitats.

Plenary

Remind the children that both plants and animals need to be able to find a place to live if they are to survive. Point out that they have considered the plants and animals that they think might choose to live in two very different habitats. They have made predictions that they will be able to check during a later activity.

Display

Divide a display area equally into two parts to represent the two contrasting habitats. Use pictures or children's drawings of the plants and animals predicted and attach these temporarily under appropriate headings. Print out statements of the predictions: *We think we will find these plants and animals living in this habitat.*

SCIENCE   CITIZENSHIP

CHECKING PREDICTIONS

Learning objective
To investigate with sensitivity predictions about the plants and animals found in local habitats.

Resources
For fieldwork – clipboard and pencil, a record of the predictions made in the previous activity. In the classroom – the children's recording from the previous activity, paper, pencils, crayons.

Preparation
Decide how best to organise this activity. If the children need to visit the sites in groups, extra adult help will be required. Make a list for the group leaders which includes the plants and animals discussed in the previous activity; allow space to mark ticks and crosses to record what is found in each habitat as the children discover them.

Activity
Tell the class that they are ready to check their predictions about the plants and animals that they expect to find living in the two different habitats. Before leaving the classroom, explain how the investigation will proceed and insist on ordered behaviour. Tell the children how the species will be recorded by the adult leading the group. Point out that habitats are the homes of plants and animals and it is important not to disturb the living things too much during the investigations. Talk about avoiding trampling on plants and not harming or disturbing animals.

At each site look for plants and animals in a sensitive, quiet manner. Perhaps each child in the group could take a turn to discover and name or describe a plant or animal. Write down some detail if possible – a shiny brown beetle, a very small spider, a yellow flower, a prickly leafed shrub.

If the weather allows, continue the activity outside. Using a record sheet from the previous activity go through the list of living things predicted and encourage the children to make comments. *We expected to find woodlice under the logs and there were many of these animals, so our prediction was correct. We did not think we would see a spider crawling over the tarmac, but there was one. This was something we did not predict.* Point out that making an incorrect prediction is not 'wrong', but can be very useful in helping to find out information during an investigation.

Ask the children if they can think of any reasons why one habitat should have more plants and animals than the other. Perhaps one area is too dry and they know that many minibeasts like to live in damp conditions; perhaps there is not as much shelter on the playing field as there is under a hedge. Help the children to understand that most animals and plants do not like disturbance, and ask them how they can help these living things to survive.

Recording
Ask the children to record what they have found out by drawing pictures to represent each habitat and to include the plants and animals they found there. They can complete this investigation by writing sentences to explain some of their predictions. Encourage them to use their recording pages from the previous activity to remind them of what they expected to see.

Differentiation
Children:
■ with help check and record predictions using drawings, investigating habitats in a sensitive manner

■ investigate sensitively to check their predictions, recording differences in habitats by drawing and headings

■ investigate sensitively, understanding the need for checking predictions, recording differences by drawings and notes and suggesting relevant reasons for differences.

Plenary
Talk about the findings from this activity. Did the children always find what they predicted? Did they discover anything they did not expect? Explain that predictions should always be made carefully, but the investigators should not always expect their predictions to be supported. Ask the children for reasons why they found more plants and animals in one habitat than the other. Point out the big differences over a small area.

Display
Rearrange the display begun during the previous activity to show which plants and animals were found in the two habitats. Include the children's statements describing the reasons for the differences.

ACTIVITY 4

LOOKING FOR IDEAS

ART & DESIGN

Learning objective
To explore design ideas through first-hand observation of natural materials.

Resources
A different collection of natural objects, perhaps relating to the time of the year (see Preparation below); board or large piece of paper for demonstrating; coloured drawing paper; paper for mounting; pencils and crayons.

Preparation
Decide upon a natural theme relating to the time of the year, which can be carried through the following two activities. In autumn focus on fallen leaves, dead stalks and seeds; in winter and early spring choose twigs with buds and use with rocks and pebbles to create stark outlines; for summer focus on the brightness of flowers, fruits and vegetables.

Activity
Refer to the children's earlier efforts at observational drawings (section 1, activity 7). Tell them that they will be continuing to practise their drawing skills and that this time there will be a different collection of things to examine. Show the class the new items. If living material such as branches and flowers is presented, explain that it has been carefully cut from the plants and only a small amount was removed; care was taken not to damage the plants or any animals living nearby. Explain the theme, then point out the special shapes, the colour range, and the different ways of looking at things. Perhaps the underside of a leaf is particularly interesting, or a vegetable more unusual when placed in a different position. Choose one of the items and trace your finger around the main shape. Explain that this is the part that could be copied first and will give a kind of framework on which to add detail. Demonstrate by drawing this outline onto a board or piece of paper and point out that you have not included every detail of the natural object but have made it more simple. Choose other items and ask the children to suggest which line could be the first to be drawn.

Next, show how some detail can be added, perhaps the veins of a leaf, a pattern on a petal, stripes and patches on a twig.

Recording

Give the children the opportunity to try these techniques for themselves. First, allow them some time to make their choice of natural object and to handle it to appreciate the texture and the shape. Then they should decide upon the angle or position from which it will be drawn. Remind the children of the stages: first tracing an outline with their finger and copying this onto the paper, then adding detail and perhaps colour. When the children are happy with their drawings, encourage them to write a separate heading that includes their name.

Differentiation

Children:
■ select and look closely at a natural object, making a simple drawing
■ select and examine a natural object, choosing an interesting aspect for an observational drawing
■ show interest and imagination when selecting, arranging and drawing a natural object.

Plenary

Talk about and admire the children's efforts. Point out drawings where particularly unusual aspects have been chosen, simple lines have been followed or colour has been used effectively.

Display

Cut out the children's drawings, leaving a border of about 1cm and then paste them on appropriately coloured backgrounds, perhaps putting similar drawings together making four or five panels themed by colour or shape.

ACTIVITY 5

LINE AND SHAPE

ART & DESIGN

Learning objective
To develop design ideas, focusing on line and shape.

Resources
A collection of natural materials as used in the previous activity; thick drawing paper or thin card; scissors; pencils and crayons.

Preparation
Cut the thick drawing paper or card into different-sized rectangles for the children's drawings.

Activity
Remind the children of their previous efforts at drawing items from the collection of natural materials. Explain that they have another chance to choose an item, examine it carefully, find an interesting way of looking at it and make a drawing. This time the drawing will be on thicker paper (or thin card) so that when completed it can be cut out accurately and the shape used as a template.

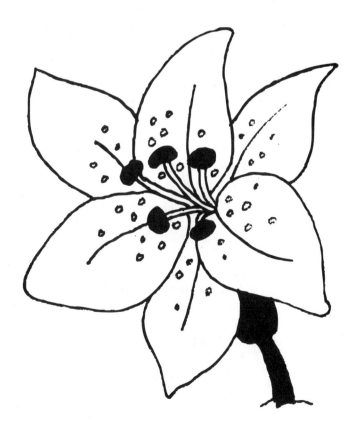

Advise making the shape quite simple and not including too much detail. Demonstrate again how to trace an outline with a finger before copying it onto the paper. Perhaps the children will find counting a help as they follow a line in small stages, and then repeating the count as they draw.

Allow the children time to select an item and examine it closely before beginning to draw. To focus their ideas, pairs of children can discuss their item telling each other why they made such a choice, which position or angle they intend to draw and the size they are aiming for.

Give each child a piece of thick paper or card. Explain that the drawing should be as large as possible – a leaf can cover most of the area, something long and thin such as a twig can stretch from corner to corner. As they draw, encourage the children to use their pencils lightly, making bold strokes and concentrating on the outline only.

When their drawings are finished, the children can cut out their shapes and write their names on the reverse. Tell them that what they have designed is a template which can be used to make many more shapes which will all be the same as their original drawing.

Differentiation
Children:
■ choose a natural object, and with help copy and cut out a shape

■ choose and examine a natural object, making and cutting out a careful copy of the shape
■ find inspiration for a design from a natural object, skilfully drawing and cutting out a template shape.

Plenary
Talk about how natural materials have given the children lots of ideas for drawing and designing; refer to the different shapes and textures that have inspired their work. Comment on the range of designs and explain how useful these will be for the next activity.

Display
Store the templates in a box or in transparent folders in a document file so that the children can compare different styles and shapes.

ACTIVITY 6

CREATING A COLLAGE

ART & DESIGN

Learning objective
To use individual design ideas to make a collective collage.

Resources
The children's templates from the previous activity; different-textured plain and patterned papers including wallpaper, packaging, wrapping paper, birthday cards and so on; scissors; Blu-Tack; glue.

Preparation

Reserve an area of the classroom wall on which the collage will develop. Choose a suitably coloured backing paper on which the children's shapes can be attached – white or pale grey will show up winter shapes, light green or blue will enhance spring and summer themes, and a neutral beige or cream would be ideal for displaying autumn colours.

Activity

Explain to the children that their design ideas from the previous activity can be used to make a large frieze for the classroom wall. Show the children where the frieze will be located. Explain that they will each use their templates to make a number of similar shapes that will be pasted onto the background to make a collage. As everyone's shape is different, the collage will be varied, but it will have a strong theme with which the children will now be familiar.

Show the children the different types of paper to be used in the making of the collage; comment on the colours and textures available. Remind them of the intended colour scheme and ask for suggestions as to which types of paper will be suitable for the copies of their design. Discuss plain colours and patterned designs. Draw the children's attention to any different textures and explain how they can help enhance the overall design. Emphasise the children's input; it is important that they feel they are directly contributing to the competed collage.

Give the children time to select the paper, draw around the shapes and cut them out. Demonstrate how to position the template on the selected paper, minimising waste, holding carefully while drawing round. If appropriate, children can work in pairs, taking turns to hold the template still while a partner draws. As their collection of shapes grows, suggest the children practise arranging them on their table to make a design, either individually or with a partner. They could try spacing and overlapping their shapes to discover different effects which might be useful when the wall display is put together.

Have an idea of how the completed design will look, but value the children's ideas and suggestions. It might be possible to incorporate both formal and random designs in the frieze. Leaves could be arranged in a swirling pattern to represent a windy day with others placed in a more formal manner as a border; winter shapes can make stark silhouettes; flower shapes can be crowded together as well as spaced out.

Attach the shapes to the background with Blu-Tack at first. Comment on the overall design and ask for the children's opinions, for example: *I think we need more plain shapes in this corner. What sort of shape would look best in this space we have left?*

Differentiation

Children:
■ with help use a template to cut out shapes and provide ideas for a collage
■ use a template to make shapes, choosing colours and textures and providing ideas for a collage
■ use a template to make shapes, carefully selecting colours and textures and contributing imaginatively to the design of the class collage.

Plenary

Refer to the collage; if it is unfinished ask for further advice. Comment on the shapes and how successfully they fit together. Point out where overlapping is an important part of the design and where spaces are effective. What do the children think of the overall effect of the colours? Are they proud of their input?

© Photodisc, Inc.

FOCUS

SCIENCE
- collecting seeds
- the variety of seeds
- seeds become new plants
- planning tests, recording and drawing conclusions

ART AND DESIGN
- observational drawings

CITIZENSHIP
- sensitivity towards wildlife areas

SCIENCE

ART & DESIGN

CITIZENSHIP

ACTIVITY 1

COLLECTING SEEDS

SCIENCE   ART & DESIGN

Learning objectives
To be aware of the huge variety of seeds; to record from first-hand observation.

Resources
A collection of seeds such as dried peas and beans, acorns and conkers, sycamore and ash keys, flower and vegetable seeds from packets to include poppy and sunflower seeds, bird seed, seeds still in pods, apple pips, tomato and melon seeds, grain and grass seeds, shepherd's purse, docks and other weed seeds; small containers to hold individual seed samples; magnifying aids; board or flip chart; paper; pencils and crayons.

Preparation
Build up a seed collection, avoiding harmful varieties such as laburnum. Be aware of any children with allergies if peanuts and other nuts are to be used. Make labels to name the different types of seeds.

Activity
Present the children with a small selection of seeds and ask them what the items have in common. They might recognise them as seeds and be able to tell each other that they come from plants and can be planted so that they will grow. Choose a seed and describe it to the class: *This seed is very small. I will need a lens to look at it more closely. It is black and round.* Then ask some children in turn to choose seeds to describe.

Next, suggest organising the seeds into groups, perhaps into three groups according to size

– large, small and those in between. Then the seeds could be sorted according to shape or colour. During the sorting, provide further examples and ask the children into which group they could be placed. Make sure the children notice any other interesting observable features of the seeds in the collection, such as a wrinkled or shiny skin, ridges or patterns of colour. Build up a vocabulary list of descriptive words and phrases that the children can use when recording.

   Point out that some seeds can be eaten – peas and beans and pumpkin seeds are part of our diet. Warn however that many seeds are poisonous and the children should not be tempted to eat anything unfamiliar.

Recording

Ask the children to make careful enlarged drawings of seeds they find interesting. Some children can add notes and labels to their drawings. Draw their attention to the name labels and the list of descriptive words and phrases.

Differentiation

Children:
■ describe a range of seeds and make simple observational drawings
■ observe closely and describe individual seeds, recording accurately with drawings and notes
■ are aware that there is a huge variety of seeds, make accurate observational drawings with relevant notes and headings.

Plenary

Talk about the huge variety of seeds, that seeds can be recognised by their differences of size, colour, shape, texture and so on. Remind the children that although many seeds can be eaten, there are others that are very poisonous.

Display

Arrange the seed collection where the children can make further observations. Encourage them to help you add to the collection. Label familiar seeds and display seed packets where appropriate. Accept that there might be seeds collected in the wild that cannot be identified.

SCIENCE   CITIZENSHIP

ACTIVITY 2

PLANTS MAKE SEEDS

Learning objectives

To know that flowering plants produce seeds; to collect material from the environment sensitively.

Resources

Different seeds still attached to part of the plant such as those in pods and cases, inside fruits and shells and so on; packets of flower seeds; pictures and books about seed production; small containers for holding seeds; envelopes; magnifying aids; camera; paper; pencils and crayons.

Preparation

Depending on the time of the year, decide if a short excursion around the school grounds or into the local

...onment would be useful for the children to observe and collect examples of plants ...ving stages in seed production. Look for plants such as the dandelion, dock, shepherd's ...e and other weeds with seed pods, blackberries and other fruits. Take close-up ...tographs of seeds found locally.

...ivity

...mind the children that there are many different types of seeds. If appropriate, refer to the class seed collection. Show the children a packet of flower seeds and ask them where they think the seeds have come from. Talk about how they were collected from plants growing in a garden or greenhouse and put in a packet for us to buy and then plant so we can have these flowers growing for ourselves. Show the children an example of seeds as part of a growing plant. Use honesty, where the seeds can easily be seen inside the seed cases, or a sunflower head, which shows the seeds developing as the flower fades. Explain that flowering plants reproduce themselves by making seeds which will grow into new plants.

If appropriate, take the children into the local environment where they can look for seeds developing on plants. Emphasise that before seeds can develop there must have been a flower. As the flower dies, the seeds begin to form. Explain to the children that some plants are weeds that grow abundantly and therefore collecting these plants is not damaging the environment too much. Other plants that are rare should not be collected or damaged.

If an excursion is not possible, provide the children with seed pods and fruits and ask them to find and collect the seeds. Provide envelopes that the children can label and decorate and use for packaging their seeds. Make sure the children understand that plants produce flowers from which seeds develop and these seeds will produce more plants of the same type. This is how these plants reproduce.

Recording

If appropriate, the children can make drawings of the parts of the plants they have collected, adding headings and labels.

Differentiation

Children:
■ identify seeds as part of a plant and know that they can produce new plants; record this by drawing and labels

■ recognise that flowers produce seeds which might be in pods and cases, and that the seeds can become new plants; record by accurate drawings and labels
■ identify seeds on different plants, know that they develop from flowers and will produce new plants; record accurately from observation using drawings and notes.

Plenary

Ask the children to remind you how flowering plants reproduce. From their experience of examining plant material, they should talk about flowers fading and seeds developing which, when the time is right, will grow into new plants.

Display

Extend the seed collection to include seed pods and cases opened to reveal their contents. Label them appropriately.

Use books and pictures as well as photographs to extend the examples. Print out statements emphasising the process of seed production and display them with arrows as a cycle:

A plant has flowers 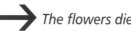 *The flowers die*  *Seeds develop*

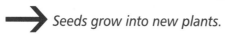 *Seeds grow into new plants.*

Seeds

ACTIVITY 3

SCIENCE

WHAT DO SEEDS NEED TO GROW?

Learning objective
To turn ideas about what seeds need to grow into a form that can be tested.

Resources
Bean seeds (peas or mustard seeds); paper; pencils.

Preparation
Decide how the tests will be carried out: the children can work in pairs and different pairs can test different needs. Prepare a vocabulary list to include *seed, need, grow, test, water, compost, root, shoot, container* and so on.

Activity
Hold a bean seed in your hand and ask the children how long you will have to wait for it to grow. Listen to all their suggestions and discuss why the bean will not grow while you are holding it. Can the children suggest what the seed will need before it will spurt into growth and make a new plant? Make a list of the children's ideas, which might include soil/compost, water, sun, warmth, a plant pot and so on.

Suggest the children think of a test they could try which would show them what a seed needs to make it grow. For example, how would they show that a seed needs water? They might think of planting seeds in different pots, watering one but not the other and waiting to see what happens. If the question is whether seeds need soil/compost, can the children suggest a method of testing this idea? Perhaps some seeds could be provided with paper, sand or fabric to see if they will grow without compost. Discuss the practical aspects of the test. What type of containers could be used? Where is a safe place to position the containers while the test is in progress? Whatever the question, how will the children know when the seed has begun to grow? What will they look for? What will they have to do to make sure the test is fair? (Use identical containers and look after all the seeds in the same way.)

Recording
The children will need to record their plan. Provide them with headings such as *What do we want to find out? What will we do? What will we need? What will we look for?* and discuss what they will write. Refer them to the vocabulary list. If appropriate, children can work in pairs, discussing their ideas and how they will present their information.

Differentiation
Children:
■ with help make suggestions for a test and record a simple plan
■ provide ideas and make suggestions for carrying out a test, recording them as a plan
■ provide ideas and suggestions for a test, understand the importance of a fair test, record a detailed plan.

ry

e children why a test is important. They should be able to talk about showing the
er to a question and ensuring the test is fair. Point out that a plan is needed so that the
s carried out in a scientific manner.

play

t out and display prominently the questions/headings to be answered.

ACTIVITY 4

PLANTING SEEDS

SCIENCE

Learning objective
To carry out a test and make sure the test is fair.

Resources
Seeds (beans, peas, mustard seeds); suitable containers – small transparent pots for peas and beans, shallow dishes for mustard seeds; compost; cling film; labels; paper; pens and pencils.

Preparation
Arrange the equipment so that it is easily available for the children to use. Decide upon the working procedure. It might be useful for a working area to be set aside for the planting with the children making visits in small groups to plant. If appropriate, prepare a set of visual instructions for the children to follow. Arrange a safe place for the planted seeds while the test is in progress but which is easily accessible for daily observations.

Activity
Tell the children they are now ready to test their ideas from the last activity. Talk about the procedure to follow and the need to work carefully and efficiently in a scientific manner.

If children are testing the need for water, they should plant seeds in two pots, using the same compost and same method of planting, and put the pots in the same position in the room. One pot will be watered each day, the other will receive no water.

If the test is whether compost/soil is needed, seeds can be planted using other materials as a growing medium, such as sand, absorbent fabric or paper. Some children might want to try more than one alternative. The seeds in this test must be all watered regularly and given identical treatment.

Emphasise the importance of a fair test so that the answer to their question is beyond any doubt. Point out the importance of labelling the pots with their names, the date and whether they should be watered or not. Cover the pots with cling film, especially over a weekend, to prevent drying out.

Recording
Ask the children to explain what they have done through drawings, labels and notes. Encourage them to say how they have made their test fair and what they will be looking for over the next few days.

CURRICULUM LINKS ages 5–7: Plants and animals

Differentiation

Children:

■ follow their plan, plant seeds and record the test with drawings and headings

■ carry out their plan, making sure the test is fair and working and recording in a ' manner

■ carry out their plan, understanding the importance of a fair test, working and recording scientifically.

Plenary

When all the planting has taken place, ask the children to remind each other what they are testing and to describe how they know their test will be fair. Talk about the next step of the investigation: that the seeds will need to be cared for and observed regularly.

Display

If possible, arrange a display around the growing seeds. Make explanatory labels and provide magnifying aids and appropriate books.

ACTIVITY 5

MAKING AND RECORDING OBSERVATIONS

SCIENCE

Learning objective

To observe and make day-to-day recordings of observations.

Resources

The containers of seeds the children prepared in the previous activity; magnifying aids; copies of a recording framework (see below); camera; pencils.

Preparation

Set aside some time each day for the children to observe the seeds and record what is happening. Arrange to take photographs as a method of recording. Prepare and photocopy a recording framework with columns for the dates and the observations of each set of seeds that the children are personally observing. Make a vocabulary list to include *root, shoot, water, compost* and so on.

Activity

Talk to the children about making their observations. Ask them what they expect to see. If the seeds have been planted in compost, talk about looking for a shoot emerging from the compost and if the containers are transparent suggest looking for roots. If the seeds are visible, scattered on absorbent material, any changes will need to be observed and recorded.

Recording

It might be useful to wait until the first sign of change in any of the seeds before beginning the recording. Then present the children with the recording sheet and indicate where they should make notes and drawings of the information they have collected from their observations. Allow the children to repeat the observations and recordings daily.

Differentiation

Children:

■ make daily observations and with help record information collected in a chart

■ make daily observations using a chart to record accurately the information collected

■ make daily observations using a chart to record accurately and in detail the information that has been collected.

Plenary

Talk about how important it is to record everything that was observed during the test. Explain that the recording will help to answer the questions asked at the beginning of the investigation, and writing all the information in a chart means nothing will be forgotten.

Display

Update the display featuring the growing seeds. Write a new label each time there is something important to record.

ACTIVITY 6

DRAWING CONCLUSIONS

SCIENCE

Learning objective

To use the results of a test to draw conclusions.

Resources

The children's tests and recording from the previous activities; the photographs taken during the investigation.

Preparation

Have available all the work from the planning to the recording of the observations.

Activity

Tell the children that now the test is at an end it is time to decide what has been found out. Their recording of the observations will help them to remember what happened during the tests. Refer to the questions that the children set out to answer. Does a seed need water before it will begin to grow? Has this been proved? Ask the children what evidence they have to show others that seeds do need water before they will grow. They have the evidence of the test, the seeds growing and not growing in their containers, and when these are no longer available there are the recording pages to show what has been observed. Ask the children if they expected the seeds to need water before they would grow.

Talk about the tests to see if seeds need compost in order to begin to grow. *Did the seeds grow when planted on paper or fabric as well as in compost? What does this tell us?* Explain briefly that compost, absorbent paper and so on are useful only for holding the water which they now know seeds need to grow. Any material that provides just enough water for the seeds would be suitable. (It might be necessary to point out that seeds given too

much water will rot before they can grow.) Ask the children what evidence they have to sho others that seeds do not need compost to begin to grow. Talk about the evidence of the growing seeds and the importance of the recording pages. Did the children think beforehar that the seeds would be able to grow without compost? If appropriate, arrange for some children to explain the conclusions that have been drawn to a parent or children from another class to emphasise the importance of what they have found out and the usefulness of the recording.

Recording

To complete the recording of their investigation, ask the children to write the answer to the question they asked at the beginning of the investigation. Some children will be able to explain in a scientific manner how they arrived at their conclusions.

Differentiation

Children:
■ with help draw conclusions using the evidence of their observations and recordings
■ understand that their observations and recordings help them to draw conclusions about the idea they have tested
■ understand the procedure of an investigation, that observations and recordings provide the evidence to help draw conclusions.

Plenary

Remind the children that they have carried out an investigation and were able to draw conclusions that answered questions they asked at the beginning. The observations and recordings were important in helping them to reach their conclusions and answer the question.

Display

Use any photographs taken to show the stages of the investigation and to add to the evidence collected. Print out and display prominently the answer to the question. Collect and present each child's individual work connected with the investigation into a folder, adding any digitally printed photographs.

ACTIVITY 7

UNFAIR COMPARISONS

SCIENCE

Learning objective

To recognise when a comparison is unfair.

Resources

Dry samples of garden soil and compost; two plant pots; two bean seeds; jug or can of water.

3

Seeds

Preparation

Leave the soil and the compost separately in shallow trays in a warm place for a few days to make sure the samples are quite dry. Label the two plant pots to show which has soil and which has compost.

Activity

Tell the children that you are thinking of extending the investigation in which they have been involved. You want to find out whether, once they have started to grow, seeds will grow

better in garden soil or in compost from the garden centre. Tell them that you think the compost is better. Show them the trays and explain that there is soil in one and compost in the second. Ask the children to help you plant a bean seed in each pot. Water the pot with the seed and compost but not the pot containing soil and seed. Then explain that you will put the two containers in a safe place and wait to see what happens.

Give the children the opportunity to question your method. They might point out that only one pot was watered. Perhaps make excuses that it does not matter. Ask the children to explain why they think you are wrong. Encourage a discussion on the fairness of the test and why the results could not be properly compared if only one pot was watered. Finally, agree that only one thing should be different if a test is to be worthwhile. In this case the difference is the growing medium; everything else should be the same – the type of pot, the amount of water and the care each seed

is given. It would not be helpful either if the pots were put in different parts of the room as giving them different conditions would be unfair. Explain that working scientifically is very important during an investigation. Unless the test is as fair as possible, the results are worthless.

Allow the children to proceed with the test if appropriate.

Recording

Ask the children to write an account of how they persuaded you to make a fair test.

Differentiation

Children:
- are aware that a comparison can be unfair
- know that the conditions of a test must be fair so that the results can be relied upon
- understand that for the results of an investigation to be of any value only one factor should be changed so that fair comparisons can be made.

Plenary

Remind the children that a science investigation is only worthwhile if the conditions are fair and only one thing is changed. If the test is fair, then the results are extremely useful when telling others what has been found out.

Display

Use any children's work to complete the seed display.

Making a collage

FOCUS

ART & DESIGN

ART AND DESIGN
- developing ideas for a collage
- looking at fabrics
- using materials and tools
- practising new techniques
- creating a collage
- developing an awareness of others' designs

SCIENCE

SCIENCE
- identifying and handling plant materials from the local environment

Preparation for section 4

The progressive activities in this section culminate in children making an individual fabric collage. The children make templates and use these to cut out fabric shapes that are attached to a background using a variety of techniques. The small pieces of work by the children can be arranged together to produce a quilt effect, a border or wall panel. Set aside a display area for the completed work and, if possible, provide a workshop space for storage and display of materials and tools required and the work in progress. Assess and avoid the risks to the children when using pins, needles and scissors.

ART & DESIGN   SCIENCE

ACTIVITY 1

DEVELOPING IDEAS

Learning objective
To use natural forms as an inspiration for ideas.

Resources
Natural materials such as seeds, fruits, leaves; drawing paper; art materials; scissors.

Preparation
Decide upon a theme for the collage, perhaps relating to the time of year with an autumn, spring or summer focus. If the children have practised observational drawings (see section 1, activity 7 and section 2, activities 4 and 5), you may want to use these examples, otherwise choose a different collection of natural materials to provide experience and inspiration.

Activity
Show the children the collection of natural materials and encourage them to talk about their impressions and share their ideas. What are the main colours? Have the shapes anything in

4

Making
a textile
collage

common? Do the shapes fall into any sort of grouping? What sort of lines can the children pick out – curved, wavy, jagged? Does the collection remind them of the time of the year, perhaps a walk in the woods, a visit to the greengrocers, a holiday incident they remember? Do any of the items go together particularly well, perhaps because of colour or a similar or contrasting shape? Pick out two or three items, describing their features and explaining why you find them interesting. Arrange them as a group in different ways, for example in a row, overlapping, at random. Make comments as you move the items around, pointing out that there is not a right or wrong way as it is a personal preference.

Give the children the opportunity to choose a small number of items and try ways of arranging them, either individually or with a partner.

Recording

Suggest the children make drawings of one or more of the items they have chosen. Build on any previous experience (section 1, activities 6 and 7; section 2, activities 4 and 5) and encourage the children to make simple lines to represent the shapes they have chosen. Point out that these shapes will eventually be used to make a collage using different fabrics. Emphasise that detail is not needed, and the simpler the shape, the easier it will be when they reach the stages of cutting out and attaching to the background. Perhaps some of the shapes need to be enlarged so that they will give greater impact to the collage. Ask the children to cut out their most successful shapes to be used later.

Differentiation

Children:
■ realise that nature can provide design ideas; draw simple shapes from observation
■ use nature as an inspiration for design ideas, drawing simple shapes from observation
■ use nature imaginatively to provide design ideas, drawing a range of shapes.

Plenary

Comment on the shapes and how they have been drawn simply, using the natural materials to generate ideas. Remind the children that this is the first stage in making a collage using fabrics.

Display

Make available the collection of natural materials so that they can be examined frequently by the children as they develop further ideas. Temporarily fix the children's cut-out shapes to the wall and refer to them when discussing the production of the collage.

ACTIVITY 2

LOOKING AT FABRICS

ART & DESIGN

Learning objective
To develop ideas for making a fabric collage.

Resources
A wide range of fabrics representing different colours, patterns and textures from which the children can select pieces for the collage; paper; staplers; pencils.

Preparation

Cut small samples (8cm × 4cm) of each of the fabrics so the children can use these for their recording. Prepare a vocabulary list which includes words appropriate to the fabric selection such as *colour, patterned, striped, shiny, thick, thin, smooth, ridged,* as well as *fold, pleat, scrunch, overlap* and so on.

Activity

Present the children with the range of fabrics and explain that these fabrics can be used for their collage designs. Encourage the children to handle and talk about the fabrics. Give pairs of children a fairly large piece of fabric and allow them a few minutes to discuss the sample. Then ask them to describe the fabric and share their ideas as to how it might be used in the collage. Do they think the colour is suitable for the theme? Are there any patterns that will enhance the design? Which fabrics have an interesting texture? Suggest the children try folding, pleating and scrunching the fabric pieces. Which ones lend themselves to these processes? Which ones will give more impact when used flat? Have they had any further ideas for their designs since handling the fabrics? Suggest they think about the shapes they made previously and which fabrics they would like to copy them on to.

Recording

Ask the children to select two or more of the fabrics that they might use in their design. Provide them with small samples of their chosen fabrics to attach to a recording sheet. Encourage them to write headings and simple notes to describe each fabric, why they think it is particularly suitable and how they intend to use each type.

Differentiation

Children:
- select and describe fabrics for a design, recording using simple vocabulary
- select and describe fabrics appropriate for a design, recording with thought and detail
- select and describe fabrics imaginatively, showing understanding of design and colour.

Plenary

Talk about the development of the design project – that shape, colour and texture have been considered. Now the children can move towards creating their collage.

Display

Arrange a selection of fabrics to be admired and handled by the children as they develop further ideas. Display the children's work in a temporary way.

ACTIVITY 3

USING PAPER PATTERNS

ART & DESIGN

Learning objective

To use paper patterns to transfer shapes onto fabric.

Resources

The children's paper shapes from activity 1; the fabric range from activity 2; scissors; soft pencils or chalks; plastic folders or large envelopes.

Preparation
Decide on the organisation of the activity and whether groups of children will work with a supervising adult.

Activity
Tell the children that now they have made drawings and chosen their fabrics, they can use the shapes as templates to create designs for their collage. Using one of the shapes and a piece of fabric, show the children how to draw around the shape using a soft pencil or piece of chalk. Perhaps ask a child to help by holding the template firmly as you make the outline. Explain that the aim is to produce a fabric shape exactly the same as the template. Carefully cut round the shape while telling the children that the simpler the shape the easier it is to cut out. Point out ways of minimising waste by careful placing of the template on the fabric.

Give the children the opportunity to select their fabrics and make their own shapes. If children are working in pairs, suggest they encourage and help each other as necessary. Provide the children with a plastic folder or envelope in which to store their cut-out shapes.

Differentiation
Children:
■ select fabric and with help, draw round a template and cut out a fabric shape
■ select fabric, draw round a template and cut out fabric shapes carefully
■ select fabric, and working independently, draw around a template and accurately cut out fabric shapes.

Plenary
Admire the shapes the children have made. Ask the children if they encountered any difficulties during this activity. Was it difficult to choose the fabric? Was one fabric easier to work with than another? Did they find the drawing round a problem? Perhaps they found the cutting out the most difficult part.

Display
Develop an area for storing the children's work.

ACTIVITY 4

DESIGNING AND MAKING A COLLAGE

ART & DESIGN

Learning objective
To consider shape and colour when creating a collage design.

Resources
Fabric to use as a background such as hessian, felt or other easily manageable material in neutral or appropriate colours; the children's cut-out fabric shapes from activity 3; pins; sewing threads; large-eyed needles; scissors; glue; stapler; extra materials for embellishment, such as padding, beads, sequins, ribbon and so on; plastic wallets for storing the work in progress.

Preparation
Cut out the background fabric into manageable rectangles for the children to work on. The pieces do not necessarily need to be the same size or colour. Plan the organisation of the activity: the children need to work in small groups with adult supervision. Depending on ability and previous experience, decide which joining techniques and embellishments the

children will use. Prepare examples of different methods of attaching fabric, such as running stitches, oversewing stitches, gluing and stapling.

Activity

Show the children the pieces of fabric to be used as background. Talk about the colours to be used: perhaps a pale colour to show up the shapes they have prepared, or a colour to reflect the time of year and so on. Use some fabric shapes and demonstrate how they could be arranged on the background. Try overlapping, leaving gaps, edges touching, positioning in relation to the edges of the fabric and so on. Make comments as you try different ideas and perhaps ask the children to make suggestions. When a pleasing arrangement has been achieved, show the children how to use pins to fasten the fabric pieces to the background. Point out that the next step will be to fix the pieces permanently to the background. Using pins means that the pieces are held in place while you work, and also enable you to make small changes if necessary.

Provide the children with the background fabric and their previously prepared shapes. Ask them to create a design, thinking carefully and trying several arrangements before finally using pins to attach their shapes.

Ask the children for suggestions as to how their pinned shapes can be more permanently fastened to the background of their collage. They might suggest making stitches, gluing and stapling. Remind them of any previous experience of sewing and show them any examples you have tried. Also show fabrics where gluing and other methods have been used. Suggest the children try different methods when making their own collage. At appropriate times introduce the children to a range of techniques to develop their collage ideas:

Sewing: Remind the children how to thread a needle and use thread to join fabric. Demonstrate how to make simple and even running stitches. Some children can try other types of stitching, such as overlapping and cross-stitching. Point out the importance of leaving enough thread to finish off securely.

Gluing: demonstrate using the right amount of glue, as well as working carefully and efficiently.

Stapling: this method can be used for fastening small or long thin pieces of fabric to a background.

Padding: show how small amounts of padding pushed between the background and cut-out shape can give a textured effect.

Pleating and scrunching: show how manipulation of appropriate fabrics can make interesting textured effects which can be fixed by stitches, glue or staples.

Embellishment: to finish off their collage, show the children how selective use of materials such as beads, threads, feathers, braid and so on can enhance their work.

The children will need several sessions to complete their collage designs.

Differentiation

Children:
- create a design and with help attach pieces of fabric to a background
- create a design, thoughtfully arranging and attaching fabric shapes onto a background
- imaginatively arrange fabric pieces and attach them to a background.

Plenary

Admire the finished collages. Point out successful examples of the different techniques used. Allow the children to feel the textures of each other's work.

Display

Depending on the finished work, find a special method of displaying the individual collages, perhaps creating a quilt effect by arranging the pieces as a block. Alternatively, the pieces could be arranged as a border around a display of the natural materials that were used to give inspiration. If space is limited, perhaps the collages could be displayed in plastic folders in a file that can be examined by children and visitors.

ACTIVITY 5

EVALUATION

ART & DESIGN

Making a textile collage

Learning objective
To review their own and others' collages.

Resources
The children's completed collages.

Preparation
If possible, display the finished collages where they can easily be seen by the class.

Activity
Start by emphasising the achievements of the children in producing their collages which contribute (or will contribute) to such a magnificent class display. Remind them briefly of the stages, time and effort taken to reach the end. Talk about highlights and difficult moments. Ask the children for their comments. How do they feel when they look at the finished work of art and their contribution within it? Discuss successful features of individual collages, perhaps where colour or shape make a special impact. Look for examples of interesting stitching, pleating, scrunching and so on. How many different examples were used? How do the textured examples complement the collages?

Talk about moving on and producing another work of art in the future. Which ideas would the children like to try again? Would they do something slightly differently? How could the same ideas be used in a different theme, perhaps at Christmas time, perhaps when making a card or decoration? Explain to the children that their ideas and experiences will help them with their next design and work of art.

Recording
Ask the children to draw a simple outline of their design and add notes, labels and comments to record their experiences of creating this particular collage. Demonstrate how a sketch can represent the collage with notes and labels written in appropriate spaces. The children could comment on the colours and shapes and identify the different techniques used. Encourage them to label their favourite feature as well as any part that gave them certain problems. To complete the recording, the children can write sentences to describe any future project they might like to try. As part of this, encourage them to refer to any successful feature they have admired in another person's collage and perhaps which they intend to try for themselves in the future.

Differentiation
Children:
■ describe what they feel about their own and others' work
■ comment on differences between their own and others' work and suggest ways of improving their own work
■ comment on similarities and differences between their own and others' work, recognising ways of adapting and improving their own work for future projects.

Plenary
Suggest the children try some of their further ideas at home. Now they have practised new skills, perhaps they could make a picture for a family member or to decorate their own room.

Display
Arrange the children's work in a box for visitors to browse.

ACTIVITY 6

OTHER PEOPLE'S DESIGNS

ART & DESIGN

Learning objective
To be aware of differences and similarities in the work of designers.

Resources
Pictures, posters, pieces of fabric and other illustrative material showing examples of designs based on natural forms from different times and cultures; items of clothing or furnishings, tableware, jewellery, and so on using designs from natural forms.

Preparation
Arrange the resource material so that it can easily be seen by the children.

Activity
Start with the children sitting where they can see the examples you have collected. Ask some children to tell you which designs they particularly like. Can they say if it is the colours or shapes that they find most interesting? Find out if the children can identify any natural forms among the designs, such as a flower or leaf shape, seed, branch or vegetable. Perhaps there are some animal shapes among the plant forms, for example a fish or butterfly. Have some of the designers chosen similar themes or similar colours? Are any of the designs rather like those the children created when making their drawings? Look for differences. Is there a design that is quite different from all the others? Perhaps it has a lot of detail while most of the others are simpler? Do the children think the designers have made any of the shapes simpler to improve the design? Perhaps they can spot a tree shape which does not have every leaf drawn, or a flower which consists of only a few lines of drawing. Point out however that the designer must have spent a long time looking carefully at natural forms for her/his work to be a success. Compare a design with lots of colour to one where colour has been restricted. Talk about the textures among the examples. Compare those that feel smooth to those where fabric and embellishments have been added.

 Talk about what the designs could be useful for. Are there any the children would like as wallpaper or curtain material? Which would they choose for using in the classroom?

Recording
Ask the children to describe two of the examples, commenting on colour, shape and overall design. If appropriate, provide small samples of paper or fabric to attach to their work.

Differentiation
Children:
■ are aware of the work of different designers and make simple comparisons
■ are aware that designers find ideas from natural forms and make comparisons
■ understand that designers find ideas from natural forms and can comment on similarities and differences.

Plenary
Point out that creative people often find ideas for their designs in nature; that a wide range of shapes, lines and colours can be found in natural forms. People in all countries have always looked around them and copied the shapes and patterns they see.

Display
Incorporate the design examples with the children's work. Print out headings and statements of comparison to link the designs.

Animals and us

FOCUS

CITIZENSHIP
- the needs of humans and other animals
- discussing and developing ideas by listening to others' points of view
- the responsibilities of owning pets
- respect for wildlife
- practical ways of encouraging and protecting wildlife

CITIZENSHIP

SCIENCE
- understanding that animals have needs
- treating animals with care and sensitivity

SCIENCE

ACTIVITY 1

WHAT DO HUMANS NEED?

CITIZENSHIP

Learning objective
To recognise that all humans have needs.

Resources
Board or flip chart; paper, pencils and crayons.

Preparation
Be sensitive towards any children living in difficult circumstances or those separated from their families. Prepare a simple two-column chart on the board, with a wider left-hand column.

Activity
Make positive comments to the class. Tell them that you enjoy their smiling faces and are pleased to see them so happy, cheerful and looking so well. Ask them what their secret is for being so happy. Is there something special they are thinking about? Do they just feel good at this minute but are not sure why? If someone is having a sad day, are they happy most of the rest of the time? Encourage the children to share their thoughts with each other.

Next, explain that there are some things which we really need to enable us to have a happy and healthy life. Perhaps some of the things the children talked about are things they want to have but are not absolutely necessary for them to be happy and healthy. Organise the children into pairs and ask them to talk to each other for a few minutes to decide which things are really important for making them happy and keeping them healthy. Suggest they decide which things they could not manage without.

Bring the class together and make a list of the children's ideas in the larger column of the chart you have drawn, grouping their suggestions so that it becomes evident that food and drink, clothes, a home with their own space, friends and family and 'something to do' contribute to happiness and being healthy. If appropriate, try to explain to the children that in their lives they probably have more than enough of the things talked about. Other people in different places perhaps have less than they do but are just as happy and healthy. Look at the list again and prompt the children into simplifying their needs. Encourage them to consider the wider human race and use the second smaller column to write key words listing basic human needs.

When talking about food, conclude that we probably have more than we need, so perhaps write *enough food* in the second column. For drink, decide that water is the most important drink for all humans; without water people die. Write a phrase to imply that simple clothing is necessary and point out that a home could mean just a shelter from the weather. Perhaps

talk about having a base, a place to go to, somewhere to be private. Identify friendship as a basic human need. Explain that for humans to be happy they need to know that other people care about them. Finally, talk about having things to do. Discuss having a sense of purpose, that humans need to be able to carry out daily activities, both when working and for enjoyment.

Recording
Ask the children to record the things they need to live a healthy and happy life. Suggest they draw themselves in a box then write words to describe their basic needs.

Differentiation
Children:
■ describe some basic human needs, recording as a drawing
■ understand that all humans have needs and record using drawings and headings
■ recognise the basic needs of humans providing detailed drawings and notes.

Plenary
Ask the children to remind each other of the basic needs of humans if they are to be healthy and happy. These are the needs of adults and children in every place all over the world. Point out that unfortunately some humans do not have all of these basic needs.

Display
Arrange pictures of a range of humans and use the children's work and printed headings to show their needs.

ACTIVITY 2

WHAT DO ANIMALS NEED?

SCIENCE   CITIZENSHIP

Learning objective
To develop ideas about animals' needs through discussion.

Resources
Pictures or models of familiar animals such as a ladybird, bird, frog, sheep, squirrel; paper; pencils and crayons.

5

Preparation
Organise children into suitable groups for discussion, if necessary with an adult supervisor.

Activity
In their small groups, tell the children you have some pictures/models/toys representing different animals. Explain that you would like them to consider the animal they are given and discuss what it needs in order to live a normal, happy and healthy life.

First, ask the children to look at the picture/toy together and think carefully about it. (No speaking at this stage.) Next, as the children pass the picture/toy around the group, the person holding it makes a suggestion as to what they think the animal needs. Then encourage further comments or suggestions from anyone in the group to develop the discussion. Allow five to ten minutes for this part of the activity, then talk to the children about recording their ideas.

Recording
Ask the children to make a small drawing of their animal in the middle of a piece of paper and to use words, phrases and drawings in the space around to show what this particular creature needs. They should try to remember what each person in their group talked about and decide whether they agree with the suggestion.

After the children have completed their recording, ask a child from each group to share their ideas and tell the others what they think their animal needs to live a normal life that is happy and healthy. Decide if the groups have reached similar conclusions.

Differentiation
Children:
■ contribute to a discussion and record group ideas as drawings
■ take part in a group discussion, recording ideas and suggestions with drawings and words
■ take part in a group discussion, recording information collected in an organised manner.

Plenary
Talk about the success of the discussions. Did the group members generally agree? What did the different groups have in common? Do the children think that they helped each other come to decisions? Point out how useful it is to share ideas.

Display
Arrange a line or group of pictures/models of animals and print out statements of their needs.

ACTIVITY 3

THE NEEDS OF HUMANS AND OTHER ANIMALS

CITIZENSHIP

Learning objective
Use a chart to compare the needs of humans with other animals.

Resources
Board or flip chart; paper; pencils.

Preparation
Draw the framework of a chart with three columns: one large and two smaller with the headings *Needs*, *Humans* and *Other animals*. Write in the needs in the larger column.

Activity

Remind the children that they have talked about the needs of humans and then considered the needs of other animals. Do they think they are the same? Perhaps some are the same but others different. One way to find out is to make a chart to compare the two.

Show the children the framework of the chart you have drawn. Explain the headings and read the words in the first column. Point out that a chart needs only a few words; sentences are not necessary. Symbols can sometimes be used. Ask the children to suggest a method of recording which will show which are the needs of humans or other animals. They might suggest using ticks and crosses or different colours in the boxes. Go through the list in the first column, deciding whether the need applies to humans and then to other animals. Ask different children for simple explanations of their opinions.

When the chart is complete, encourage the children to make comments. *Are the needs of humans and other animals exactly the same? What are the differences? Did you expect greater differences? How similar are we to other animals in what we need to live a normal life in a happy and healthy way?* Together, devise a conclusive statement to compare the needs of humans with those of other animals.

Recording

The children can choose an animal and explain what it needs, making comparisons with their own needs. Encourage them to use the chart for information.

Differentiation

Children:
■ help to complete a chart and make simple comparisons between the needs of humans and other animals
■ use a chart to compare the needs of humans and other animals
■ understand the purpose of a chart, and how it can be used to show similarities and differences between humans and other animals.

Plenary

Ask the children to summarise what the chart shows. Explain that at a glance it is possible to find out what humans need and what other animals need and to compare the two.

Display

Arrange the chart together with the children's work from the previous activities.

SCIENCE   CITIZENSHIP

ACTIVITY 4

ANIMALS AS PETS

Learning objectives

To understand that pets need to be looked after; to treat animals with care and sensitivity.

Resources

Pictures and books about pets; board or flip chart; photocopiable page 56; pencils and crayons.

Activity

Talk to the children about pets. Decide what a pet is: an animal that lives with humans and needs to be looked after by its owners. Ask the children which animals they know can be kept as pets. Make a list to include dogs, cats, rabbits, hamsters, goldfish, budgerigars and

5

so on. Avoid emphasising exploited tropical and wild creatures that are sometimes kept as pets, such as snakes, other reptiles, birds and so on. Explain that pets are used to living with humans, unlike wild creatures. They rely on humans because they are not used to looking after themselves. Talk about having responsibility and what it means in relation to a pet. Discuss the characteristics of a pet, that it should be friendly, not too big, and will become part of the family. Refer to the pictures and books relating to pets.

Ask the children what a pet needs to live a happy and healthy life. Refer to previous activities and include the following points in the discussion:

1. Food – the right type and amount.
2. Water – a plentiful supply of clean water.
3. Shelter – most pets need their own special, safe place to sleep, especially somewhere warm when the weather is cold.
4. Freedom to behave naturally – pets need enough space of their own to act normally and should be given regular exercise if appropriate.
5. Care – owners have a responsibility to look after their pets, keeping them clean, cleaning up after them, making special arrangements and visiting a vet if the pets become ill.
6. Respect – explain that taking on a pet gives a person the responsibility of looking after it in a caring and understanding way, as well as providing it with its everyday needs.

Recording
The children can name and draw the pet described on photocopiable page 56.

Differentiation
Children:
■ are aware of the needs of pets and know that humans have a responsibility to look after them
■ are aware of the needs of pets and recognise the responsibilities humans have towards them
■ are sensitive to the needs of pets and understand the responsibilities of humans towards these animals.

Plenary
Point out that pets have needs, as humans do. When people decide to own a pet it is therefore their responsibility to make sure that the pet is provided with everything it needs.

Display
Create a pets corner with pictures and toys. Include pet accessories and leaflets on caring for pets.

ACTIVITY 5

LOOKING AFTER PETS

CITIZENSHIP

Learning objective
To be aware of the responsibility of owning pet.

Resources
Soft toys/models to represent pets; pictures of familiar pets; pet care accessories, such as feeding and drinking bowls, leads, small animal homes; a class pet if appropriate; paper; pencils and crayons.

© Nova Developments

Preparation
Be aware of children without pets. Ask the children beforehand to bring a photograph or drawing of their own pet or one belonging to a grandparent or other relative. Children without a pet can 'adopt' the class pet or use a soft toy for this activity. Decide whether the children will discuss in groups or as a class.

Activity
Choose some children to talk about their pets, describing appearance and habits. Then move on to discussing the specific needs of different pets. Encourage the children to talk about the right amount and the right type of food that their pet requires. How do they make sure that water, which is essential, is easily available for the type of animal? Which is the most suitable container? What sort of home does the animal need? Small mammals need somewhere clean and safe, with a warm sleeping area and plenty of room to behave normally. Dogs, of course, need regular exercise outdoors.

Encourage the children to discuss the care their particular pet requires. All animals need respect from their owners. Explain that this means providing them with their needs and taking special care of them, treating them kindly and allowing them to behave naturally. Some types of pet, such as dogs and cats, need the companionship of humans. All pets need to be kept clean, groomed as appropriate and their living spaces cleaned out regularly. Point out the responsibility of dog owners to clean up any mess their pet leaves behind. Talk about pets becoming ill and requiring the special care a vet can provide.

Recording
Ask the children to write about their responsibilities as a pet owner. Ask them to name and draw their pet. Provide them with headings, such as *Food, Water, Shelter, Exercise/natural behaviour* and *Care*, under which they should provide information in the form of words, phrases or drawings relating to their pet.

Differentiation
Children:
■ are aware of their responsibilities as a pet owner, recording with words and drawings
■ recognise their responsibilities as a pet owner, recording the needs and care required by a particular pet
■ understand their responsibilities as a pet owner, recording comprehensively the needs and care required by a particular pet.

Plenary
Remind the children of the considerable responsibilities of keeping a pet and talk about some of the problems that might be encountered, such as going on holiday, pet or owner becoming ill, people losing interest in a pet. Point out that there are situations where it is a good idea not to have a pet.

Display
Develop the pets corner, adding the children's work.

5

Animals
and us

CITIZENSHIP

ACTIVITY 6

ALL ANIMALS DESERVE RESPECT

Learning objective
To be aware that humans have a responsibility to ensure the well-being of animals, including minibeasts.

Resources
Pictures and reference books of a range of British wild animals such as hedgehog, owl, stickleback, frog, ladybird, bumblebee, bat, beetle, woodlouse and so on; board or flip chart; paper; pencils.

Preparation
Write the sequence of questions on the board so the children can refer to them as necessary (see below).

Activity
Show the children a picture of a British wild animal, perhaps a frog. Refer to the sequence of questions you have prepared, and with the children's help write down their ideas. Have a reference book available to encourage the children to check any disputed facts.
■ What is its favourite food? (For example, flies and slugs.)
■ Where does it like to spend its time? (In ponds and damp places.)
■ What is it most afraid of? (Large birds, cats and humans.)
■ Why is it important to humans? (It eats garden pests.)
■ What is this animal? (A frog.)
Perhaps use another example, this time a minibeast such as a beetle.
   When the children understand the pattern of the activity, organise them into pairs and provide each pair with a picture of an animal. Ask them to think of suitable answers to the questions. Make books available for the children to research information.
   Next, collect the children together and choose individuals to describe the animal they studied, without giving its name. Ask the rest of the class to identify the animal. Throughout the discussion, emphasise the need for wild creatures to live undisturbed, especially by humans. Point out their need to find food for themselves and perhaps their young, and to hide from danger. Talk about ways in which humans can respect these animals, such as avoiding damaging their habitats, not removing them from their natural environment, keeping away from their homes, not frightening or damaging them. Encourage the children to develop a respect for all creatures.

Recording
Suggest the children record their answers, arranging the information on a chart or as a booklet.

Differentiation
Children:
■ develop an awareness of their responsibilities towards wild animals
■ begin to understand that as humans they have a responsibility towards all animals
■ understand that as humans they have a responsibility towards all animals and are aware of ways wild animals can be helped and respected.

Plenary
Point out to the children that they share the environment with a range of wild creatures, many of them much smaller than themselves. Remind them of their responsibilities towards

all animals and how they should help rather than damage or destroy the animals and their habitats. Emphasise that helping can mean not doing anything because keeping away and not disturbing creatures is important.

Display
Arrange pictures of familiar animals together with the children's answers.

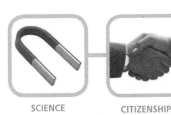

SCIENCE   CITIZENSHIP

ACTIVITY 7

HELPING WILD ANIMALS

Learning objective
To understand that there are ways for everyone to show their responsibilities towards local wildlife and habitats.

Resources
Pictures of animals to be found in the local environment, such as small mammals, insects, spiders, other minibeasts; board or flip chart; paper; pencils.

Preparation
Write or print out 'messages' to prompt discussion during the activity: *Do nothing*; *Put out food*; *Grow special plants*; *Make a pond*; *Pile up logs*; *No litter.* Seal these in an envelope or small box for the children to open. Perhaps invent a character who could have sent the messages to help the children respect and value the plants and animals of their locality. Think of a name for the character which connects with that of the school, street or nearby area familiar to the children.

Activity
Remind the children that they share the local environment with many different animals as well as a range of plants. Point out some of the attractive features of the locality that can be enjoyed, perhaps a park, an area with footpaths, a pond or stream, a patch of trees. Explain that these areas are the homes of many animals even though the animals might not always be visible. Talk about areas of the school grounds where animals might like to make their home. Refer to any pictures of animals you have.

Next, introduce the children to the invented character, providing a verbal description of this character, perhaps with a simple cartoon-like drawing. Explain that the character has lots of ideas for helping the wildlife of the area and has sent some messages to use. Introduce the messages one by one, encouraging the children to discuss what they might mean.

Do nothing: leaving areas undisturbed and doing nothing can be important. This allows creatures of all kinds to live their lives normally. Animals which are frightened or have their homes damaged will move away or perhaps die if they cannot find food or shelter. Baby animals, such as birds, will die if deserted by frightened parents. Killing and harming animals by thoughtless behaviour can be avoided. Removing animals such as frogs and fish from their natural environment can disrupt their lives often causing death.

Put out food: some animals can be helped by food being provided; talk about putting out food for birds.

© Photodisc, Inc.

Grow special plants: providing plants which caterpillars, butterflies and bees prefer as their food supply helps them to survive.

Make a pond: a pond provides a habitat and food supply for water-loving animals that could not live in dry places.

Pile up logs: a log pile provides a home for small creatures which live to live in dark places.

No litter: everyday litter and other rubbish increases the danger for animals by trapping and perhaps poisoning or choking them.

Together, devise some concluding statements, for example:

1. Everyone can avoid disturbing and killing animals and leaving litter around.
2. Most people can put out food for the birds, especially in winter.
3. Some people might have space to grow special plants, make a log pile or even dig a pond.

Recording

Ask the children to write out some rules of behaviour for themselves to follow in places they know wild animals live. Remind them that this includes very small creatures. Ask them to include any positive ways in which they might encourage wild creatures into their garden if they have one.

Differentiation

Children:

■ begin to develop an understanding of their responsibilities towards wildlife in the locality

■ identify where wild animals can be found in the locality and understand some of the ways in which humans have a responsibility to wildlife

■ identify the habitats of wild animals in the locality and understand ways in which wildlife can be protected and encouraged.

Plenary

Point out that the children have discovered many things that they can do to help protect the wildlife in the local area. Emphasise the importance of helping wild animals, and that this is the responsibility of all humans.

Display

With the help of the children, create a picture of the character and print the advice he gives.

ACTIVITY 8

SCIENCE   CITIZENSHIP

WILDLIFE AREAS

Learning objective

To develop ground rules for wildlife areas.

Resources

An area within the school grounds that can be designated as a wildlife area; paper; pencils and crayons.

Preparation

If a wildlife area already exists, familiarise yourself with the types of habitat it provides and the animals that live there. Otherwise create a wildlife area, which can be as simple as a pile of logs, a beetle bank, an area of rough grass, a patch of garden, a bird feeding station. Plan an excursion around the school grounds for the children to identify suitable places that could be developed as wildlife areas.

Activity

Remind the children that it is important to encourage and protect wildlife; that wild animals need areas of their own where they can live undisturbed. Explain that it is a good idea for people to create special areas to encourage wildlife, as many habitats have disappeared. Most people like to have hedgehogs, birds, bees, butterflies and other creatures in their gardens. Suggest that the ground around the school can be used as a special wildlife area. Ask the children for their ideas: *Where are the best places for wild animals to make their homes?* Draw attention to any parts of the grounds already designated as wildlife areas.

Before taking the children outside, talk about appropriate behaviour – that everyone must respect any wildlife already nearby, trampling and damaging plants can be avoided if people are careful and thoughtful.

Outside, identify the wildlife areas or suitable places that could be set aside for wild creatures. Talk about making a pile of logs or a bank of soil to encourage minibeasts, planting extra trees or shrubs to provide cover and perhaps food, setting up a bird table, cultivating a garden.

Recording

Ask the children to record their own ideas for encouraging more wild animals into the school grounds. Suggest they identify a suitable location and make a simple plan with drawings and notes. They should describe the creatures they hope to attract and explain how the area will be kept safe and undisturbed. Explain that the children and adults in the rest of the school will need to know about the wildlife area and how to treat it.

Differentiation

Children:
■ begin to appreciate that humans have a responsibility towards animals and describe some of the ways they can help; become involved in a practical way
■ are aware that humans have a responsibility towards animals and suggest ways of encouraging and protecting wildlife; help with a practical project
■ understand that humans have a responsibility towards animals and their habitats and can describe ways of encouraging and protecting wildlife; make positive contributions to a practical project.

Plenary

Point out the importance of the children's contributions to encouraging and protecting local wildlife. Explain that all humans have a responsibility to help wild animals and show them respect. Praise the children's present and continuing efforts within the school grounds. Consider how interesting it is for us all to share the school grounds with other types of animals. Talk about respecting wildlife wherever they are: at home, when round and about their neighbourhood, when on holiday.

Display

Create a special on-going wildlife display, perhaps with the help of older children in other classes. Have a bulletin board to record sightings and a diary for monitoring animal and plant activity. Frequently refresh the display by adding pictures, questions, puzzles and competitions so that children will keep referring to it. Encourage children to write their own reports relating to local wildlife.

Animals as pets

Can you recognise these pets? Name and draw them.

Which pet...
- likes to be taken for a walk
- sometimes needs brushing
- loves to chew meaty bones?

Which pet...
- needs a warm, safe shelter
- likes food such as carrots that it can gnaw
- needs its home cleaned out often?

Which pet...
- needs material to make a cosy bed
- needs toys to help it exercise
- needs a home safe from bigger animals?

Which pet...
- will curl up to sleep anywhere
- likes milk, fish and meaty food
- can be very friendly?

Animals and their young

FOCUS

SCIENCE

SCIENCE
■ reproduction and growth in the animals to be found in the local environment
■ using secondary sources

CITIZENSHIP

CITIZENSHIP
■ sensitivity towards animals

SCIENCE   CITIZENSHIP

ACTIVITY 1

ANIMALS PRODUCE YOUNG

Learning objectives
To be aware that animals in the local environment produce young; to understand that animals need safe places to rear their young without being disturbed.

Resources
Pictures and reference books of familiar animals and their young; photocopiable page 60.

Activity
Remind the children of some of the animals that can be found in the locality, referring to previous activities as appropriate. Explain that as animals grow older, they have young ones that grow up and in turn have young of their own. Talk about the animals needing safe places in which to lay their eggs or produce young, and where the young can survive.

Show the children a picture of an animal to be found in the local environment, such as a snail. Briefly talk about where a snail might live and where the young snails might grow up. Tell the children that young snails look like their parents but are smaller. They live in spaces among stones and other dark places, coming out to feed on plants at night. Move on to other examples, perhaps a hedgehog, bird and spider. Point out that each young animal grows larger and becomes an adult itself.

© Nova Developments

6

Animals
and their
young

Then choose an example where the young creature does not resemble the adult and show a picture of a butterfly or a frog. Ask the children to name and describe the young of these animals. Emphasise how different the caterpillar/tadpole is from its parent, but as it grows up it will change and become like its parent, then produce young of its own.

Explain that all these creatures need their own special places in which to grow up into adults and have their own young. Point out that many animals do not look after their young for long, if at all, and this is normal behaviour. However, these creatures still need a safe environment if they are to grow and become adults.

© Getty Images/Yuri Shibnev

Recording
Ask the children to record some of the animals and their young which share their environment with them. If appropriate use photocopiable page 60, where the children are asked to draw and describe the young of four named animals and then choose two animals of their own.

Differentiation
Children:
■ are aware that wild animals living around them grow up and have young; show this as drawings
■ understand that all animals, including those living in the local environment, grow up and have young; describe this with drawings, words and phrases
■ understand that all animals, including those in the local environment, grow, change and produce young as they get older; record a range of examples with drawings and notes.

Plenary
Remind the children that they themselves are growing and changing as they get older. Similarly, other animals living in the local environment are growing and changing. These creatures need safe habitats where they can produce young of their own. Refer to the part children can play in helping animals grow up.

Display
Add the children's work to the displays that developed from the activities of section 5.

SCIENCE   CITIZENSHIP

ACTIVITY 2

YOUNG BECOME ADULTS

Learning objectives
To describe the changes from young to adult using secondary sources; to be aware of the specific needs required to complete a life cycle.

Resources
Video film and reference books showing the development stages of a specific animal, which could be a butterfly or moth, frog or familiar bird; paper; pencils and crayons.

Preparation
Decide on the animal to be studied, which might depend on the resources available.

Activity
Show a video film that traces the development of the animal chosen for study. Then ask questions, such as *Where does the animal like to live? What is its main food? Where does it lay its eggs? Are they well hidden? What happens when the eggs hatch? Do the parents take care of their babies?* (Birds yes, butterflies and frogs no.) *What do the young eat? As they grow, how do they change? Do they just get bigger or is there a more dramatic change?* (For example, caterpillars and tadpoles.) Consider how a life cycle might be disrupted by careless humans. Discuss removing frogspawn, harming butterflies or disturbing baby birds.

Ask some children to tell the story of the development a stage at a time. Perhaps number the stages to aid memory, for example:

1. Butterfly lays eggs on leaf.
2. Eggs hatch.
3. Tiny caterpillars feed on leaves.
4. Each caterpillar grows bigger and bigger.
5. Caterpillar turns into chrysalis.
6. Butterfly comes out of chrysalis.

Recording
Ask the children to describe using sentences and illustrations the development of the animal.

Differentiation
Children:
■ recognise the changes in the development of a familiar animal
■ describe the stages in the development of a familiar animal, using information from appropriate reference material
■ describe in detail the stages in the development of a familiar animal, using appropriate reference material.

Plenary
Point out that the animal can only develop if it has a safe place to live and a good food supply. Remind the children of ways they can protect and encourage this animal – not disturbing the nesting site, not thoughtlessly damaging the habitat and so on.

Display
Use pictures showing the life cycles of familiar animals to include with the children's work.

Animals
and their
young

Young animals

Draw and describe the young of these animals.

snail	bluetit

butterfly	frog

Choose two other animals and draw and describe their young.

Display

It is important to display as much as much of the children's work as possible. Making their efforts available for others to see not only adds value and prestige to what the children have achieved, but also emphasises the importance of any information they have collected, ideas they have had and explorations they have made.

If children know that their work will be valued and available for others to examine, they will take more care over presentation. At this stage of their development, the habit of always producing their best efforts is worth encouraging.

Individual presentation

Collect each child's individual paper work – drawings, completed worksheets, written pieces, plans and so on – and present them in a folder or as a booklet, which they can personalise and show to each other and their parents/carers. Examples of art and craft work can be contained in a pocket attached to the folder. If necessary, any pieces of work needed for classroom display can be photocopied for the children.

Provide photocopies of diagrams and photographs of animals and plants, which the children can add to their work to give the folders or booklets an extra dimension.

Classroom display

The themes and colours of the displays will be determined by the time of the year in which the activities take place. The seasons each provide their own distinctive atmosphere, which should be reflected in the displays.

Begin to build up a display as soon as the work on *Plants and animals* begins. The displays will evolve over the weeks as the work progresses.

It can be useful to display each child's work relating to a specific activity in a temporary way, perhaps with Blu-Tack, so that discussion and evaluation can take place and the work can be admired. Make sure the work is on a level where it can easily be seen by all the children.

Where appropriate, photocopy and enlarge examples of individuals' work to use with a particular display.

If space is limited, extend the display into the corridor or school hall.

Frequently refer to the displays as the topic develops, reminding the children of the different elements of their work and the progress they are making, and noting connections across different areas of the topic.

Suggestions for display for each section
Plants and animals in the local environment

■ Create a display that reflects the local environment, particularly the area where the fieldwork takes place. Perhaps cut out typical tree shapes, representations of a familiar plant or a landmark.

■ Start with pictures and headings of the plants and animals to be found in the local environment. Add to these any photographs taken during the fieldwork activities. Provide a statement to emphasise that discoveries were made at first hand. Include the children's work – their drawings, charts, worksheets and so on.

Display

■ Print out some of the code statements from section 1, activity 5 and display them prominently.
■ Arrange the collected natural materials where they can be examined, and incorporate some items in the wall display. Use the children's observational drawings with their headings, as well as any photographs of their individual arrangements.

Our environment

■ Display pictures and photographs of different types of habitats. Divide a board to represent the two contrasting habitats studied. Include pictures showing the plants and animals the children expect to find there. Print out statements of the children's predictions. Rearrange the board as the predictions are checked and add further statements explaining what has been discovered.
■ Depending on the time of the year, create a themed collage using the children's cut-out shapes.

Seeds

■ Make an arrangement of as many different seeds as possible – seeds in packets, in pods and cases, and attached to plants. Add books and pictures and the children's drawings. Include statements describing the processes of seed production.
■ Reserve a display area to give importance to the on-going investigation. Include the questions to be answered, the growing seeds (which do not need light so do not have to be near a window), explanatory labels, recording of the observations, any photographic sequence, statements of conclusions reached, children's other work, books, magnifying aids and so on.

Making a collage

■ Organise a workshop area to accommodate the materials and equipment needed for the activities in this section. Include a storage system for the children's work as it progresses.
■ Display fabrics for handling and examination, with a vocabulary list of descriptive words and phrases.
■ Reserve a display area for the finished collages; these can be arranged in a block or as a border around the natural materials that provided the inspiration for the designs.
■ Incorporate examples of other people's ideas where natural materials have provided inspiration – pieces of fabric, wallpaper, cushion designs, other household and clothing examples, also images on postcards and in books.

Animals and us

■ Cut out pictures or draw a group of representative humans and arrange around them statements and the children's work relating to their needs.
■ Arrange pictures of pets, farm animals and the wildlife of the local area, (perhaps in a long line in contrast to the human group) and print out statements relating to their needs.
■ Use the chart to compare the needs of humans and other animals.
■ Create a pets corner to display the work about the children's pets; include photographs, toys and pet accessories. Print out statements emphasising the responsibilities of owning a pet.
■ Devote a special display to encourage a positive attitude to the wildlife of the area. Include photographs and pictures of the plants and animals to be found there, the children's ideas for preserving the wildlife and any code of conduct devised.
■ Create an on-going display to raise the profile and monitor the school wildlife area. If appropriate, incorporate work from other classes in the school.

Animals and their young

■ The work from this section can be added to the display 'Animals and us'.

Assessment

At the end of the topic *Plants and animals*:

SCIENCE
- Can the children recognise and name some familiar plants and animals found in their local environment?
- Can they identify and compare nearby habitats?
- Are they aware that there is a wide variety of seeds?
- Do they understand that flowering plants produce seeds which can become new plants?
- Do they know that, like humans, plants and other animals reproduce?
- Can they observe and learn from first-hand experience?
- Can they record and communicate what they have discovered?
- Do they make and check predictions?
- Can they follow the procedures of a scientific investigation?
- Do they recognise an unfair comparison?
- Do they treat the environment with respect and recognise where there might be hazards?

ART AND DESIGN
- Can the children make relevant and careful observational drawings?
- Can they use natural materials to explore design ideas?
- Does their work communicate their ideas of line, shape and colour?
- Do they use materials and tools efficiently?
- Do they collect visual and other information to develop their work?
- Have they applied learned techniques to produce a finished work of art?
- Can they handle fabric successfully to create a collage?
- Do they recognise ways of improving their designs and moving forward with their work?
- Do they appreciate the designs of other people and comment on similarities and differences?

CITIZENSHIP
- Do the children recognise that humans have needs?
- Do they understand that pets, farm animals and wildlife also have needs?
- Have they developed a greater awareness of their local environment?
- Do they demonstrate sensitivity and respect towards the plants and animals in their environment?
- Do they recognise their responsibilities to all animals?
- Can they identify some of the plants and animals of the local area and talk about ways of helping to encourage and protect wildlife?
- Are they able to take part in discussions with another person and the whole class?
- Do they take an interest in and discuss local and topical issues?

Drawing the topic to a close

Look back with the children at what has been achieved throughout the work on *Plants and animals*. Point out how much they have learned, all the things they have discovered, the information they have gathered, and the enjoyment they have had. Remind them of the fieldwork activities, the observations they made and any special encounters they experienced. Emphasise how much more familiar they now are with their surroundings and the plants and animals that share their environment.

Ask the children which part of the topic they have enjoyed the most and which piece(s) of work they are especially proud of.

Refer to the scientific aspects of the topic, the importance of careful observations, the success of the investigation. Comment on any on-going efforts the children are making to encourage and safeguard wildlife. Point out that their ideas and thoughtfulness can be extended to their own gardens and other places where there are plants and animals. Help the children to see that all they have learned and discovered about the needs of humans and other animals is relevant to their wider world and for the rest of their lives.

Talk about the children's artistic achievements – the collaborative collage, as well as their individual efforts. Relate any positive comments made by other children and teachers or by visitors to the classroom.

Arrange a simple but special event as a finale. Invite parents and carers to look around the classroom to admire the children's achievements. Enlist pairs of children to act as informative guides to explain the different aspects of the work, how the scientific investigation was carried out and how the ideas for the artwork were developed.

Suggest the children write down questions about plants and animals on small pieces of paper and post these in a suitable box. To round off the topic, help them to organise a quiz, perhaps with individuals selecting questions at random for others to answer.